Executive Career Advancement

How to Understand the Politics of Promotion

The X Factor

by

Lorenzo G. Flores, Ph.D.

www.LFCareer.com
Phone (559) 222 - 6307

authorHOUSE™

1663 LIBERTY DRIVE, SUITE 200
BLOOMINGTON, INDIANA 47403
(800) 839-8640
WWW.AUTHORHOUSE.COM

First published by AuthorHouse 11/20/2009

ISBN: 978-1-4208-0756-1 (e)
ISBN: 978-1-4208-0755-4 (sc)

Printed in the United States of America
Bloomington, Indiana

This book is printed on acid-free paper.

Dedicated to
Javier, Teresa, and Jennifer
Make A Difference

Table of Contents

Chapter 7

Chapter 8

Preface

We are much beholden to Machiavelli and others,
that write what men do, and not what they ought to do.
Sir Francis Bacon

I want to get promoted, but I don't want to play the game. This statement reflects the fact that most people want to move up the career ladder but are unsure of how to deal with the political end of career advancement. Unfortunately, career advancement is not a do-it-yourself program. While it may look like advancement can be achieved by individual effort, it actually requires the push and pull of influential people and special interest groups, getting someone to the top. People seeking advancement often decide that they must move into the zone of promotion politics. Intuitively, they know that career advancement is too important to be left in the hands of management. They realize that there is too much at stake to leave the discussion of career politics at the level of office gossip.

How This Book Can Benefit You

This book promotes the development of better career decision-making skills through an understanding of promotion politics.

The concepts in this book will give readers a mental frame of reference that will allow them to discuss career advancement as they would any other matter of organization business. For example, what implications does career advancement politics have for leadership? When someone is promoted to an executive position, do we get the best leader, the best politico, or a hybrid? The politics of promotion plays an important but largely overlooked role in leadership. Very likely, executives would not be in their leadership positions if they did not have a working knowledge of the politics of promotion. People committed to career advancement understand that hard work alone will not get them promoted.

All politics are based on the indifference of the majority.
James Reston

Maintaining A Healthy Work Environment

**The dynamics of career advancement are critical
to the leadership and management process.
They go to the heart of morale, productivity,
and control in the work environment.**

Not discussing career advancement politics makes it highly conspicuous by its absence. We are uncomfortable with the sometimes messy details that accompany the politics of power. It is easier to be enthralled with the latest bandwagon leadership techniques and catchy buzz words. Not to mention fire walking for building self-confidence and executive wilderness survival skills. Unfortunately, as well intended as these are, they are sometimes misused in an attempt to answer the deeper questions about the personal politics and the promotion practices of making it to the top. A new level of appreciation is needed for the complexities that surround career development.

True Grit

**While extolling the virtues of hard work, this book takes
on the tough subject of promotions politics. It takes an
unflinching look at the critical role that politics plays in
shaping careers.**

For example, if we know that some of our beliefs about career advancement are not exactly accurate, why do people continue to promote them? Do they lack information or are they in denial? The aim of this book is to encourage intellectual curiosity and create a more level playing field by eliminating negative promotion practices. This is done by presenting conceptual models that help people approach career politics in a more informed way.

Things may come to those who wait,
but only the things left by those who hustle.
Abraham Lincoln

One reason so much misinformation regarding career advancement exists is that many people have not been encouraged to think of career advancement in any way other than what has been taught to them at home, in school, in the military, or in the office. That is: performance is all that counts. As homilies go, the idea that "performance is all that counts" has a nice ring to it. It evokes images of being promoted after years of working strenuously in the organization's vineyards. Although it conjures up mental pictures of one making it on his or her own, it conveniently skips over the dark side of executive performance as it relates to the politics of promotion. Many executives need to examine their relationship to this idea. The truth be known, in the world of executive career climbing, the notion that "performance is all that counts" doesn't come close to describing what a person has to do to become "king of the hill" and maintain that position. To move ahead in a positive way, we need to respect the hard work ethic. We also need to build on this value in order to create a higher level of understanding.

Pushing The Envelope
of
Career Advancement Knowledge

No training needs assessment is complete without questions about career advancement politics.

Today's workforce wants a level playing field. Employees want to know about the formal and informal sides of moving up the career ladder. Therein lies the uniqueness of this book, which sets forth a framework for discussion and expands the boundaries of information available about the politics of promotion.

The ability to tap into the business, social, and political sides of one's career is critical to achieving a higher position. Since most people want to advance, it is imperative that they invest time in understanding the forces that shape their careers. Thus, we need to find the right words and be cognizant of perspectives that enable us to present our ideas.

*Safeguard your position by practicing defensive
and offensive career strategies. Lorenzo Flores*

Career Advancement Dynamics, and the politics of promotion represent a major piece of working knowledge missing from the big picture of career development. This book provides constructive ways to fill in these information gaps. Sometimes executives attempt to fill in the void by stressing hard work, leadership, and teamwork skills. One must master these topics, but also be adept at career politics in order to survive the pressures from competitive peer rivals. On many levels, the book gives a voice to people who might not otherwise have a way to analyze and change the organization's promotion practices.

Career Advancement Dynamics:
An Essential Discipline

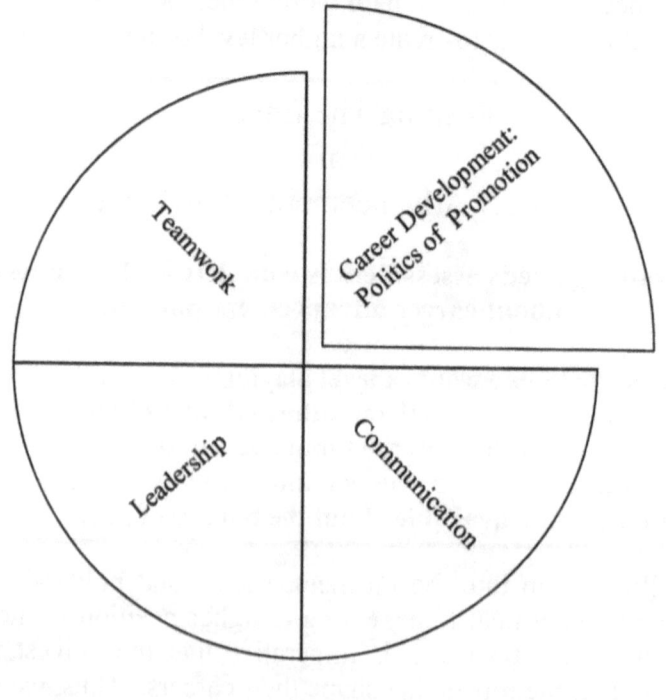

Introduction

I do not believe such quality as chance exists.
Every incident that happens must be a link in a chain.
Benjamin Disraeli

For many high-reaching people, the American dream includes career advancement. They realize that they have about thirty years to make it to the top, or at least to some position near the top. Unfortunately, to make this dream come true they must travel down the rocky road of Career Advancement Politics. In spite of their hard work and honesty, many people feel betrayed when they wake up in the middle of the American dream and realize that their chances for a place at the top are slipping away. Sooner or later, everyone must come to terms with the rigorous realities of promotion politics.

The Cardinal Rules Of Career Advancement

1. **There is no substitute for hard work and working the politics of the organization.**

2. **Don't trust anyone who says that politics never played a role in his or her promotion(s).**

This statement underscores the point that no one makes it to the top without knowing how to deliver quality work and how to manage the public and private aspects of career advancement. It's not whether or not you play politics it is a question of degrees–how much do you play politics? This book looks at new approaches to discussing the complexities of career advancement politics and the human condition as found in the workplace. Readers will develop insights that will help them determine if they have the stomach to do what it takes to reach the top. To this end, the main sections of the book focus on:

- **The Theory and Practice of Career Advancement**
- **The Real World Model for Career Advancement**
- **The Conventional Wisdom Models for Career Advancement**
- **The Surreal Model for Career Advancement**
- **The Multi-Cultural Promotion Track Simulation Game**

The beginning of wisdom is the definition of terms. Socrates

Dynamics of Career Advancement: How to Understand the Politics of Promotion

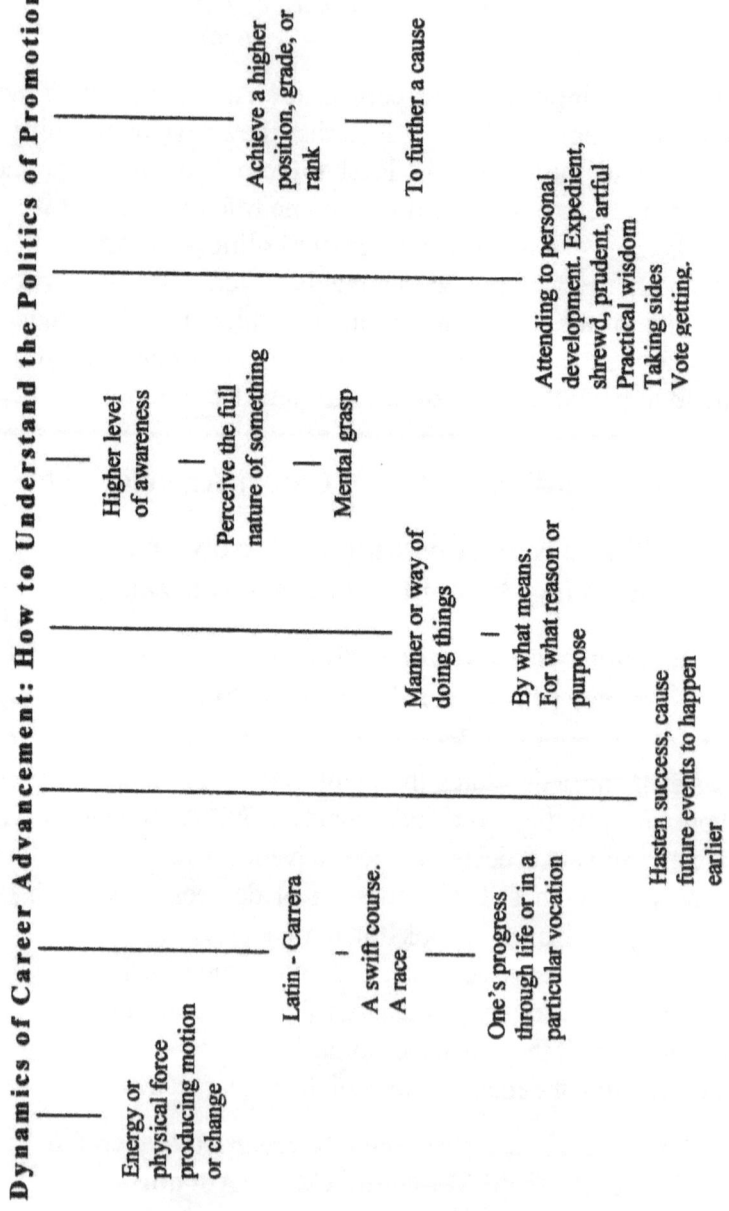

Energy or
physical force
producing motion
or change

Latin - Carrera

A swift course.
A race

One's progress
through life or in a
particular vocation

Hasten success, cause
future events to happen
earlier

Manner or way of
doing things

By what means.
For what reason or
purpose

Higher level
of awareness

Perceive the full
nature of something

Mental grasp

Attending to personal
development. Expedient,
shrewd, prudent, artful
Practical wisdom
Taking sides
Vote getting.

Achieve a higher
position, grade, or
rank

To further a cause

And God created the Organization and gave It dominion over man.
Genesis 1, 30A, Subparagraph VIII

More than ever, career advancement requires a meeting of the minds and souls of workers and managers. This is because the workplace is often filled with competitive egos and minefields. As hard as organizations try to make things fair, fairness does not always work the way it should.

Playing With Dynamite

Career Advancement Politics can be useful or dangerous. The sparks fly when the workplace is politically charged. Therefore, career politics must be closely studied and carefully handled in order to achieve breakthroughs.

In order to move up, you must have an action plan and be able to execute it. With this in mind, this book offers perspectives that can be helpful in career decision making. The more information and assessment skills people have, the better they will understand themselves, the dynamics of the workplace, and their chances of reaching the executive level. Most people begin their careers with an ideal of what it takes to climb the career ladder, but no one really knows what is expected of them until they begin the ascent to the top. People who want to advance in today's competitive workplace must be prepared to deal with people who are hard working and honest and people who are hard working but have flexible ethics. By all standards, career advancement in competitive organizations has a logic all its own, a logic that requires:

- **Professional work skills**
- **Exceptional politicking skills**
- **New concepts for understanding advancement**
- **Critical thinking skills**
- **Commitment to cultural diversity**

These points make the text a catalyst for discussing the changes needed to maintain a healthier work environment.

The fierce dragon of promotion politics has wings and claws and breathes out fire and smoke, but its soft underbelly can always be pierced by common sense.
Lorenzo Flores

Secrets Revealed

All of us progress in our careers, but some of us advance more quickly and further than others. Some say promotion is due to performance. Others claim it's due to connections.

What do you say?

Explain _____

The above question may seem controversial or like an idea whose time has come for dialogue. Either way, as organizations change and the work force becomes more diversified, the need for informative insights into career advancement politics becomes more critical. So, why not gather this information together in an understandable format, design a social action framework, and operationalize the concepts so they are accessible to everyone?

Executive Promotion
The Nature of the Beast

Promotion politics is a living, breathing entity with an insatiable appetite for competitive success at any cost. It feeds off self-interest, self-preservation, and self-promotion. It breeds convoluted rules for career advancement. The fact that it is a reality and a necessity for career survival makes it a formidable force to be reckoned with in the workplace.

Even the hint of prejudice of any type
has no place in a well run organization. Fred A. Manske, Jr.

In the land of career advancement--politics is king. As a discipline, career advancement sets forth concepts that focus on what it takes to move through the ranks and make it to the top. This includes an interest in the racial and gender divides that exist in the executive suites. It asks the question "Why do so few people of color make it to CEO?" It seems that for a female or person of color to make it to the top he or she must pass through the eye of the needle.

Do Some People
Pay a Higher Price for Their Ambition?

Do people of color and women lack the wherewithal to be CEO? Or is there something built into the infrastructure of the organization that resists or resents the transfer of power to them?

Without a doubt, the issues that make up the politics of promotion represent a great deal of unfinished business that needs to be discussed. In many ways an organization's progress and morale level are in direct proportion to its ability to discuss and resolve issues related to career advancement politics. Leaders and staff must learn to better handle these issues and leave a positive legacy for the organization and the generations that follow.

Medieval Censor
The Dark Ages of Career Advancement

Unless we shine a light on the politics of promotion, future generations will believe we sabotaged our own potential by self-imposing childlike taboos that prohibited the discussion of career advancement politics.

Executive training programs that avoid analyzing the politics of promotions are by default: (1) Shortchanging people who want political assessment tools, (2) minimizing the role of politics, (3) protecting the status quo, and (4) closing systems to new ideas.

Career Shaping Questions

Judge a man by his questions rather than by his answers. Voltaire

Healthy organizations seek outside reality checks. We must ask questions that suck the marrow out of hard core issues and hidden agendas--so that we can know how things are done. At the end of chapters 1 through 10 the reader will find threshold questions for career advancement that are essential to surviving and thriving in the workplace. There are over 160 consciousness-raising questions that engage the reader at a deep introspective level of thought and action. Without career advancement critical thinking skills, a person is at the mercy of promotion sharks who know the intricate value of hard work and politics. The critical thinking questions serve to fill in the information gaps surrounding the politics of promotion that often exist between staff and management.

How to Use the Career Shaping Questions

1. Sometimes there are so many political complexities that we might not know what career development questions to ask. If this is the case let the book ask the thought-provoking questions for you. For example, make a statement like "In the book the author says such and such about career advancement. What do you think?" This allows the text rather than you to become the focus.

2. Review the questions from a training needs assessment perspective. Answer all the questions or choose those of interest to you or your work group. Study groups that meet before or after work may be a consideration. The idea is to start dialoging and doing critical thinking about career advancement politics and how the questions apply to you and your workplace.

3. For maximum benefit the questions should be answered together with the boss. If answering questions with higher-ups is not possible, answer them individually or with a group of co-workers. The text will be useful to anyone (students to executives) interested in career advancement dynamics.

4. Assess your responses and formulate a practical plan of action for career advancement and dealing with the politics of promotion.

Career Shaping Questions

You'll never have all the information you need to make a decision.
If you did, it would be a foregone conclusion, not a decision.
David J. Mahoney Jr.

Whether the questions are used by students or working professionals, they have the power to drill through hard core issues. The questions can flesh out the exacting answers that can save a lot of precious time and energy. Answering these questions also teaches a person the importance of challenging one's personal assumptions and beliefs. Somewhere out there, there is someone who received extraordinary help (see Extraordinary Mentoring pp. 76-79) moving up the career ladder but is smug enough to say that he or she made it on his or her own. And there is someone else who is arrogant enough to think that he or she doesn't need anyone's help to make it to the top. These two need to put aside their false sense of pride and have an honest discussion about the intrinsic role of hard work and politics. If the history of career advancement were to be written, it would be evident that career advancement is an artful discipline that most people are left on their own to learn. Promotion politics has become incredibly challenging, fluid, and perplexing.

No Time for Self-Complacency

Career advancement is not what it used to be; just to keep your position, not to mention advancing, requires pro-active political thinking and action.

This book, combined with its captivating quotes, career shaping questions, and candid photos (a picture is worth 1000 words) provides an edge in making career decisions and appreciating the complexity of career advancement. It also introduces the one-of-a-kind Multi-Cultural Promotion Track Simulation Game (pp. 245-253). As a package, these are powerful tools that can help alter an organization's promotion practices and enhance a person's view of what it takes to get ahead. In many cases, the Human Resources Department is the best source of information for career development and cutting edge insights into organizational changes.

Career Shaping Questions

There are no inappropriate questions.
There are only inappropriate answers. Sixty Minutes

Only the Paranoid Survive

Andrew S. Grove

The competition can be beguiling, hard as nails, and ruthless. It is always calculating to stay three steps ahead of the uninitiated newcomer to career advancement politics.

It's OK to assess the boss's work style, strengths, and vulnerabilities, because he or she is evaluating the pluses and minuses you bring to the workplace. By familiarizing yourself with the threshold questions, you can stay ahead of the learning curve, which is a major factor in progressive career advancement. If you don't do this, you can bet your smiling competitors will. By answering the questions readers will personalize the book and be more attuned to:

- **Assessing the organization's culture and promotions practices. Thus, avoid underestimating how complex career advancement can be.**

- **Analyzing the boss and anticipating how he or she might feel about promotion politics and how he or she can help or hinder your career.**

- **Identifying your strengths and weaknesses. Check your information sources and challenge assumptions.**

- **Critical thinking that enhances problem-solving and decision-making. Answer the career shaping questions by going with your first feeling. This way you will beat the temptation to give middle-of-the-road responses when your true beliefs and experiences are different.**

Compelling Quotations

Quotations are true levelers. They give, to all who will faithfully use them, the spiritual presence of the best and greatest of the human race.   William Ellery Channing

This book contains over 225 right-on-the-mark quotes that can stimulate dialogue and strategies regarding the politics of promotion. Many executives have mastered the secret of using mind riveting quotes that make a point, spark new ideas, and win over the opposition. Hard work combined with a quick wit, penetrating insights, and a polished personal style can boost your professional image. Whether it is a one-liner or it contains several lines, a quote can provide a sharp competitive edge. Clearly, the ability to cite quotes that have survived the test of time and debate is a powerful career enhancement tool.

Introduction to the Multi-Cultural Promotion Track Simulation Game

The expense isn't what it cost to train employees. It's what it cost not to train them. Philip Weber

Do you dare enter the belly of the beast? In addition to presenting groundbreaking concepts, this book features an introduction to the Multi-Cultural Promotion Track Simulation Game (pp. 245-253). This hands-on-training tool picks up where this text leaves off. It enables participants to walk in someone else's shoes (African American, Asian, Hispanic, White female, or White male) and try to make it up the career ladder of a fast-paced organization. The mind-opening simulation gives the participants a you-are-there experience from the perspective of true-to-life competition for promotions and the trade offs involved in achieving career success. The educational game lends new insight into the inner character of competitors and the idea that it is lonely at the top and crowded at the bottom. As a marker for change the Human Resources Department may use this educational tool to create transparency and maintain positive relationships between management and staff.

Career Shaping Questions

1. **What is your career goal? Select one of the following:**

   Supervisor_____   **First level manager**_____

   Middle Manager_____   **Executive level**_____

   Chief Executive Officer _____

   Other: _____

2. **The last time you were promoted, to what did you attribute it? If the question does not apply to you, how do you feel that people are promoted?**

   Select one of the following:

   Hard Work _____   **Politics** _____

   Hard Work and Politics _____

   Other: _____

   Explain:_____

3. **How do you define Career Advancement Politics?**
   Explain_____

4. **How does your boss define Career Advancement Politics?**
   Explain_____

Career Shaping Questions

5. **What do you know now about Career Advancement Politics that you wish you had known before you started your career?**

    Explain_____

6. **To what extent should staff have a working knowledge of career advancement politics?**

    Circle your choice

    None 1   2   3   4   5   6   7   8   9   10 Great

    Explain_____

7. **Should training needs assessments measure the staff's demand for information regarding the politics of promotion?**

    Circle your choice

    No   1   2   3   4   5   6   7   8   9   10   Yes

    Explain_____

8. **If the politics of promotion plays such an important role in executive career advancement, why is it not studied and openly discussed?**

    Explain_____

Chapter 1

Career Advancement Politics:
A New Discipline

Conventional Career Wisdom
vs.
Real World Career Realities

*If you make people think they're thinking, they'll love you;
but if you really make them think, they'll hate you.*

Don Marquis

Blast-off for Success

Hard work is the launching pad, but
politics is the rocket fuel of career advancement.

Got rocket fuel?

Career Advancement Politics:
A New Discipline

Every truth passes through three stages before it is recognized.
In the first it is ridiculed,
in the second it is opposed,
in the third it is regarded as self-evident.
Arthur Schopenhauer

Knowing the parts of the formal and informal organization is one thing; knowing how they relate to one another is the essence of promotion politics. In a reality-based work environment, it is crucial to have A to Z insight into the organization's promotion practices. In this sense, career advancement dynamics provides a theoretical framework that enables people to pose questions that go to the heart of career advancement. It is important to understand career advancement from the inside out. And to ask penetrating questions that flesh out career politics by using a format that answers the vital questions: who, what, when, where, why, and how things are done. In a straight forward way this book pioneers a new school of thought regarding the politics of promotion and your career.

The discipline of Career Advancement Politics can assist in the following ways:

Provides Transparency

Assess and anticipate problems

Promote a pattern of predictable behavior

Foster greater learning, teaching, and research

Ensure efficiency in carrying out the organization's goals

Provide a sense of control over promotion process and practices

Career Advancement Politics:
A New Discipline

People need the protection of promotion and evaluation
procedures that diminish the importance of internal politics.
Judith M. Bardwick

If career advancement was a straight forward process there would be no need for the applied principles of Career Advancement Theory.

Career Advancement Dynamics offers a large body of knowledge that places a sharp, laser beam focus on the methods that are used to promote people. Because it is supported by a solid conceptual base, the subject cannot be discounted by people who feel that politics has no bearing on promotions. Career Advancement Politics recognizes that people who want to advance up the career ladder need to integrate certain principles into their thinking and acting. The conventions regarding personal and professional relationships must be examined, perhaps redefined in light of today's workplace realities. This is important, because understanding relationships is critical to learning how management and individuals work together to achieve mutually beneficial goals. Concepts like the X Factor, leadership, preselection, hard work, and preferential treatment may coexist or crossbreed together in an organization's culture and must be dealt with in a respectful way. There is a need for models that zero in on promotion issues which confront people during their career. Appreciating career politics, as defined below, is essential to a person's advancement.

Career Advancement Politics

The ability to blend hard work with the art of playing with appearances, emotions, and words.

Career Advancement Theory

Men like the opinions to which they have become accustomed from youth; this prevents them from finding the truth, for they cling to the opinions of habit.   Moses Maimonides (1135 - 1204 A.D.)

The definition of Career Advancement Politics on page 5 highlights the reality that working hard is only part of the career advancement story. The other half is an abstract art that requires the ability to improvise and seek out opportunities for advancement. This book brings to the forefront innovative skill sets that can be taught and learned. Career advancement is no longer a topic that is off limits for discussion or analysis. It is an engaging subject that, when approached in an attentive way, gives answers that people need in order to make positive choices. Most people feel that they control approximately 80% of their career advancement potential, specifically, productivity, attitude, and punctuality. The remaining 20% is comprised of factors controlled by a person's superiors. The ratio may not be 80-20. One side may be higher or lower. The important truth is that no individual controls 100% of his or her career advancement. To understand the big picture of career advancement politics you must see it through political eyes. Keep one political eye on the organization's promotion practices and the other political eye on the organization's promotion process. Things get shuffled around quickly before your very eyes. You must sort out what part is real and what part is pure con game.

Ye Olde, Executive Shell Game

If management knows what factors are under a staff member's control, does the staff member know what aspects of his or her career advancement are under management's control?

No one but management knows for sure what aspects of career advancement they control. However, it is not unreasonable to think that managers have executive privileges that they are at liberty to use. These prerogatives enable them to take risks and make judgment calls that are comfortable to them. Executives always stack the deck of cards in their favor.

Career Advancement Theory

Those in power codify their privileges into laws. Paul Eldridge

In other words, management has the last word in a lot of things that impact a person's career.

Life is unfair to people who do not have the power to define fairness.
L. Flores

What forces outside your control determine your career advancement?

Example _____

Given that management has the final say on who to promote, it is important to focus on the factors that impact careers. The Politics of Promotion must be raised to a full level of awareness so that a higher order of thinking can occur. Until now, the only models available for analyzing the sociopolitical aspects of career advancement have been the Conventional Wisdom Models (pp. 103-175). These are well intentioned, but they are largely the inventions of executives and managers who are in positions of power and influence and can tell people what they ought to do to advance as opposed to telling them what it really takes to advance. When it comes to defining fairness and how the promotion system functions, it appears that the powers-that-be have taken a lot of liberties with the realities that make up career advancement. Clearly, there is room for new perspectives that can serve as catalysts for reform by examining the factors that impact advancement. In order to piece the promotion puzzle together, this chapter introduces the Theory of Career Advancement, which asks the proverbial questions, "How do you move up?" and "How do you rate with the boss?" The following pages explore the rating system and political stealth tools used by some executives to decide who to promote to top positions.

7

Career Advancement Theory

*You know you are paying your dues when you endure personal
discomforts in order to get into the boss's comfort zone. Lorenzo Flores*

Executives view things through a prism of politics and recognize that necessary behavior cannot always line up with a company's traditions. There is a difference between traditions and behavior. While executives extol the organization's traditions they also realize that for the sake of the organization's survival they must sometimes deal shrewdly with people. This requires executives to fine tune their political skills and employ political tools to control people underneath them.

**Political Tools
In the World of Executive Promotions
A Person's Rate Of Advancement Depends On:**

1. Performance..............................**as defined by management**

2. Potential....................................**as defined by management**

3. Likeability................................**as defined by management**

4. Personal skills...........................**as defined by management**

By screening people through these criteria, a manager promotes the person who comes closest to matching his or her ideals. The four points noted above make up the X Factors that higher-ups use in their promotion calculus. Depending on the executive's need and state of mind, these criteria may be measured by either one of the following yard sticks:

Objective...**Free of bias and prejudice**

Subjective.......................................**Based on personal
                                                              attitudes and feelings**

No person is 100% objective. People can be only as objective as their life-long biases permit them to be.

1

Performance as Defined by Management

If I were objective or if you were objective or if anyone was,
he would have to be put away somewhere in an institution
because he'd be some sort of vegetable. David Brinkley

Staff members who develop competency and expertise are seen as people who have mastered the responsibilities of their positions. They're viewed as dependable and exceeding the technical aspects of their jobs. By continually upgrading their skills and doing everything that superiors have told them to do, they have become proficient in their field.

Keep the Faith - What's Left of It

An objective conclusion would be that the person who is the most competent at his or her job would be moved into top management. However, in the world of executive promotions, management applies its own logic to evaluate people and decides who fills the plum jobs.

Career advancement is about hard work and a person's ability to fit in with management's promotion practices. Sooner or later the boss will want to know how loyal you are. Plus, what you think about the organization's promotion practices. What follows is a series of questions (asked over time) and paradoxes designed to reveal your true colors. Careerist know that there are two ways to answer questions, the wrong way and the organization's way. This makes up the "I've -got-you in my pocket" test, which must be passed with flying colors. Oftentimes, when a person is dismissed, the reasons given pertain to an inability to acclimate to the organization's culture or to actively support the boss's philosophy as it pertains to business strategies, management styles, and promotion practices. The issue is integrating the boss's work style into your work style. This permits the boss to see that the two of you have similar values and that you grasp the way he or she thinks. This is why it is important to have several ways of finding out from the boss how you are performing on the job.

2

Potential as Defined by Management

Those who rule us are like you and me. It's a frightening situation.
Brooks Atkinson

Who is CEO material, or as some bosses say, who is executive timber? Many individuals have all the makings of an executive, but will be allowed to rise only to middle management. Deciding who has the inherent capacity for executive development is left up to top management. Everyday, executives answer the question of who is CEO material by the way that they demonstrate their predilections for certain types of people. They exercise their special prerogatives by granting privileges to some and not to others.

How Do You Rate with the Boss?

Some people are advanced on potential alone; others have to prove themselves over and over.

Agree _____ Disagree _____ Other _____

Explain _____

Advancement is not a matter of whether a person has potential; it's a matter of whether the boss perceives one as having the potential he or she is seeking at a given moment in time. In other words, advancement is not so much a matter of talent as a matter of opportunity. Management has its own way of defining potential and identifying who it will promote. When management identifies someone as a potential executive, it gives "the chosen one" the opportunity to rise up the career ladder. Thus, measuring someone's potential is a highly subjective exercise. Management judges people on the bases of its uniquely constructed perspectives, standards, needs, and the reality of the moment.

3

Likeability as Defined by Management

You're obviously suffering from delusions of adequacy.
Alexis Carrington "Dynasty"

Often times, an unconscious motivation to seek a personal level of comfort and safety accounts for our preference in friends and values. Perhaps it's a primeval human instinct for security that drives us to like some people more than others. Therein lies the substance of what is termed *likeability*, which is a personal choice practiced by everyone.

The X Factor
in
Career Advancement

**Do higher-ups like you enough to promote you
to a position where you can compete against
them for promotions?**
L. Flores

The X Factor is the perfect political stealth tool because it can be anything that appeals to the boss from A to Z. Appearance to Zeal for one's work. The boss decides what the X Factor(s) will be. After all is said and done, it comes down to comfort zone reality. People who remind the boss of himself or herself have greater chances for advancement. Plainly, there is a direct correlation between likeability and how often one is promoted. The flip side of likeability is discrimination. Many people have not outgrown their fear of those who are different from them. They have somehow managed to preserve prejudicial vestiges from the past. Discrimination, whether done with malice or through a casual remark, results in someone being denied an opportunity for advancement. At best, the practice may cause an unintended slighting of people. At worse, it is rooted in racist attitudes, gender bias, homophobia, and antipathy for older workers.

4

Personal Skills as Defined by Management

The prejudices of ignorance are more easily removed than the prejudices of interest; the first are blindly adopted, the second willfully preferred.
                                                            George Bancroft

All politics are personal. This refers to the distinctive skills that an individual has to offer beyond his or her professional talents. These are formal and informal signature traits that allow people to add personalized touches to their interactions with others. Someone may be a natural-born conversationalist and negotiator or he may have acquired talents such as sports and hobbies.

Ambitious Politicos Never Sleep

If personal relationships were not important, up-and-comers would not pay attention to the boss's outside interests.

Some people develop the same interest and skills as the boss (e.g., golf) so they can participate on the same level. Career social climbers take more than a passing interest in knowing what cuisine, liquor, make of car, and personal passions excite the boss. With a little effort, these can be rated, ranked, and exploited in order to "get-an-in" with the boss.

Career Advancement Is Self-Inflicted

Lorenzo Flores

There is no limit to the personal skills that can be cultivated to get under the boss's protection plan. While some describe developing such skills as "kissing up," others redefine it as preparing oneself for advancement. They consider politicking to be a skill that enables them to develop special ties that, when combined with hard work, bind people together via mutual interests.

4

Personal Skills as Defined by Management

*You have to have your heart in the business and
the business in your heart. Thomas J. Watson, Sr.*

The decision to use any personal approach to create or maintain
a personal relationship is strictly a matter of conscience. In other
words, "Can I live with this decision?" People in touch with the
complexities of career advancement know that professional skills
alone will not get them to the top. The same goes for personal
skills.

Practice Until It Becomes Permanent

**A healthy complement of
professional "can do" thinking and a personal
"aim to please" attitude is critical for advancement.**

Pinpoint and develop the areas you have in common with the boss.
A dedicated careerist is always looking for ways to tactfully mix
and match his or her talents and skills with those of the higher-
ups. In most situations this should be done in an inconspicuous
but meaningful way, barely noticeable, but yet complementing the
boss's style. This enables the careerist to get in good with the boss,
or at least get in and be seen as a supporter with common interests
and talents that can make life easier for the "big guy." Like wizardry,
this places the career climber in a position to work his magic and
parlay his or her talents (e.g., sports, knowledge of the arts and
sciences) into opportunities and contacts. It also helps if you get the
boss out of the office and into neutral territory. This permits you to
study him or her when out of his or her power element. This type of
interpersonal relationship can be continually nurtured as a means of
attaining information and promotions. This gives new meaning to
the phrase "You reap what you sow."

It also lets you see to what degree the boss views people as mere
corporate entities or as unique human beings with feelings and
needs.

Summary

Occasionally, a man must arise above principles. Warren Buffett

Career Advancement Theory addresses the fact that any discussion about promotions must be broken down into two parts: the process and the practice. Many times people do a better job of describing the promotion process than they do of explaining the organization's promotion practices. The promotion process consists of the formal policies for advancement. They include the steps that can be observed in creating a candidate list and interview panels. All of these are handled in a professional, up-front manner.

Career Advancement Ethics:
"Are They Reality or Fiction?"

Usually, there is nothing wrong with the promotion process. It's the promotion practices that are what need to be reformed.

True ____ False ____

Explain _____

The promotion practices are the underpinnings for the way that many things get done. They consist of a bifurcated system of formal and informal methods. On the formal written and spoken levels, the promotion practices and procedures appear well thought out and worker friendly. They make up an impressive package that enables the organization to proclaim its commitment to having a level playing field. Were it not for the existence of the informal shadow organization and its penchant for hidden agendas and double standards, these well-scripted formal statements would make an ideal description of the promotion process. However, human nature makes its presence felt through the informal promotion practices, by which management takes its prerogatives to promote the types of people it wishes to advance. Human nature in career advancement refers to the personal and professional traits that sway people to do right or wrong as they climb the career ladder.

Summary

A person usually has two reasons for doing something:
a good reason and the real reason. John Pierpont Morgan

Ego Trip?

A leader would not be a complete leader without the ability to exercise his or her prerogatives.

How sweet a thing to wear a crown. Shakespeare

Emboldened by these intoxicating prerogatives, mangers can justify their hiring and promotion decisions by stating that they are "pulling in" the talent needed by the organization. The longer people are managers, the more proficient they are likely to be at disguising and exercising their preferences for people who remind them of themselves. This brings one to the reality that the promotion process is more labyrinthine than some people are prepared to admit. It is complicated because it is hard to detect at which point a manager is applying his or her prerogatives in a formal or informal manner. For fairness to occur, the promotion process and practices must complement each other and be open to full examination.

A Chilling Effect on People

If the promotion process and promotion practices are out of balance, a level playing field does not exist.

Consequently, a leader's credibility is always on the line and is often the first victim of informal promotion practices. When this occurs, it takes seemingly countless acts of high level executive honesty and transparency to overcome one act of dirty politics and regain the staff's full trust.

Career Shaping Questions

X Factor

An unknown quality or qualities that determine how far and how fast people move up the career ladder. Only management knows what subjective traits are preferred. A code of silence prevents full disclosure of these prerogatives.

Example
Hard work + Competency + X Factor = Promotion

1. **List X Factors that influence the boss's decision on who to promote. E.g., connections, socializing, former co-workers.**

   _____

   How are the X Factors working for you? _____

   How are the X Factors working against you? _____

2. **How does management seem to define employee potential?**

   _____

   List the formal aspects of employee potential - a matter of record.

   _____

   List the informal aspects of employee potential - off the record.

   _____

Career Shaping Questions

3. How does management seem to define employee performance?

Explain _____

List Formal Aspects of Performance
(On the record)

_____   _____

List Informal Aspects of Performance
(Off the record)

_____   _____

4. How do higher-ups seem to define employee likeability?

Explain _____

List Formal Aspects of Likeability
(On the record)

_____   _____

List Informal Aspects of Likeability
(Off the record)

_____   _____

Career Shaping Questions

5. How do higher-ups define employee personal skills?

_____

6. List the formal aspects of employee personal skills.

   On the record - formally speaking

   _____

   List the informal aspects of employee personal skills.

   Off the record - informally speaking

   _____

7. Are executives ready, willing, and able to create a fair and level playing field for people (Black, Brown, White, gay, female, etc.) who are qualified to become CEO's? Is it in the CEO's interest to create a level playing field or does it go against their interest?

   Circle your choice.

1	2	3	4	5	6	7	8	9	10

   Yes, executives have   No, executives do not
   it in them to create a   have it in them to create
   level playing field.   a level playing field.

   Explain _____

Career Shaping Questions

8. Describe the differences between:

Promotion practice: _____

Promotion process: _____

9. How would you reconcile the differences between the promotion process and the promotion practices?

_____

10. How does it feel to win on a playing field that has never been level?

Explain _____

11. How does it feel to lose on a playing field that has never been level?

Explain _____

12. Human nature at work. List 4 things you have learned about people and their workplace behavior.

1. _____ 2. _____

3. _____ 4. _____

How does this effect your attitude towards career advancement?

_____

Chapter 2

The Real World Model
for
Career Advancement

*The best way of making your fortune is to let people
see that it is in their interest to promote yours.*
Jean de la Bruyere

Pssst! Want to Know a Secret?
Your Real Competitors Are Father Time
and Mother Nature

Your inner clock is ticking. In the race against time, hard driving,
ambitious people want to make it to the top as young as possible.
The age range for CEO's is 45 - 65. If you can survive to age
sixty without health problems you are a walking miracle.

Impress people the right way and leave your
mark so you will be remembered come promotion
time. That's what getting ahead is all about.

Learn to control the career clock though self-
discipline, patience, and timing.

Introduction
to
The Real World Model for Career Advancement

The first and great commandment is don't let them scare you.
Elmer Davis

Politics is hard work! Odds makers say that the chances of anyone making it to CEO, based strictly on a hard work ethic and no politicking, are nonexistent. This is because everyone has political blindspots they must identify and overcome. To beat the odds, a person must be able to reason conceptually about the promotion paradoxes that dwell within the workplace.

How to Deal with Workplace Paradoxes

Know your limits
Focus on your goals
Stay flexible and balanced
Learn every loophole for every rule
Decide what decisions you can live with
Come to terms with the true facts of the workplace

By shortening the learning curve, a person can increase his or her rate of career advancement. The learning curve, or "learning the ropes," is the name given to the formal and informal education process that organizations use to teach people how to do their jobs and what is expected of them. Because there is so much to "catch on to" in a short amount of time, the learning curve requires a higher level of reasoning. In real time analysis careerism calls for thinking at the speed of career advancement politics.

Introduction to
The Real World Model for Career Advancement

If others could only see us as we think we are. Ken Hubbard

"Stay ahead of the learning curve" is the mantra of fast paced organizations. The pace is quickened by the fact that there are two sides to the learning curve that have to be simultaneously understood: the formal side and the informal side. Employees are rated and ranked on how quickly they learn their jobs and on how well they develop a feeling for the organization.

Formal Learning Curve
Basic work skills
Intermediate work skills
Advanced work skills

Informal Learning Curve
Deference to authority
Innate resourcefulness
Emotional stability

Persons seeking advancement must work both sides of the learning curve. This means thinking at the velocity of promotion politics, which come at a high rate of speed. To do this effectively and efficiently, a person must meet the learning curve test that stresses the following attributes:

Envisioning
Anticipating situations before they occur.

Assessing
Remaining poised, ready to improvise. Sorting out formal and informal factors.

Positioning
Gaining advantage by tactfully benefiting from planned and unplanned events.

Learning and Applying
Adapting to changes smoothly and looking for innovative ways to stay ahead.

The Real World Model
for
Career Advancement

A mind stretched to a new idea never returns to its original dimension.
Oliver Wendell Holmes

Outstanding career advancement progress requires that a person continually analyze the politics of promotion and keep them in perspective or face being caught off guard. The Real World Model analyzes the promotion practices and questions the Conventional Wisdom Model's assumptions about what it takes to get ahead. The Real World Model provides concepts for discussing common career advancement issues across various lines and levels in the workplace. This model is all about self-empowerment and the reality that a person's rate of advancement is only as good as his or her ability to analyze and work with the organization's promotion practices.

What Price Favor and Power?

Nowhere like in the workplace are a person's ethics, principles, morals, and values challenged on a daily basis.

Example _____

Resolving these issues calls for a higher order of thinking, which empowers one to deal pro-actively with multi-faceted career paradoxes. The diagram on page 32 depicts the five steps of the Real World Model. Below each step are troublesome promotion paradoxes, which a person must reconcile in his or her own way. The paradoxes reflect that career advancement is made up of a lot of moving parts which must be constantly aligned, balanced, linked together, and centered. This speaks to the fact that there is no promotion process free of internal contradictions. Each step is discussed in detail so that the reader can better appreciate the issues that impact a person's career.

Trust everybody, but cut the cards. Finley Peter Dunne

Career paradoxes are the bricks and mortar of decision making for advancement in today's workplace. Generally, the promotion process is rife with issues and uncertainties that manage to tangle people up in difficult situations. These paradoxes are part of the landscape that continually test a person's resolve by placing him or her on the horns of a hard-hitting dilemma.

The Devil Is in the Paradoxes

The fact that paradoxes produce conflicting emotions makes them the perfect instrument for shaping careers, modifying behavior, and achieving hidden agendas.

Example _____

A paradox requires a person to simultaneously hold in his or her mind two contradictory points of view. The individual must select one over the other and consistently support that decision in spite of any contrary feelings he or she may have. Promotion paradoxes are on-the-job tests that are used by management to determine how far people will be allowed to advance. There is no end to the way clever executives can use paradoxes to track progress or compare one person to another.

Let the Games Begin!

Paradoxes, whether manufactured or circumstantial, are used to gauge a person's political savoir faire and overall usefulness and potential.

Without a doubt paradoxes signify the defining moments that make or break a person's career. The trick is to pace yourself and not peak out too early. Don't be too good too early. Always leave room for improvement.

> *Bureaucracy defends the status quo long past the time*
> *when the quo has lost its status. Laurence J. Peter*

As a comprehensive concept, the Real World Model breaks new ground by analyzing the promotion paradoxes and questioning the assumptions about what it takes to move up. Don't assume that because your skill sets work at one level they work at the next level. Career advancement requires new skill sets for every new position. From this perspective the Real World Model provides a forum that can assist in the following ways:

- **Explores the rites of promotion passage**
  To get promoted, what is expected from a person formally and informally? How reasonable are these expectations?

- **Looks at short and long range issues of upward mobility**
  Weigh the trade-offs. Immediate vs. delayed gratification.

- **Assesses management's accountability in the promotion process**
  Identify the organization "shot callers" and how they operate. How accountable are they for a person's career development?

- **Examines how workers can better prepare themselves for advancement**
  How do you hold yourself accountable for your career development?

X-Ray the Organization

**The Real World Model can be used to assess the organizational practices that control careers.
It provides a cognitive framework that allows people to reason conceptually about the politics of promotion.**

"Why do you want to become president?"
Because that's where the power is! John F. Kennedy

In comparison to the Conventional Wisdom Models (pp. 103-175), which will be discussed later, the Real World Model puts forth an alternative perspective and a systematic process for discussing the discipline of career advancement. This is important because there comes a point in everyone's career when he or she realizes that hard work alone will not move him or her up. The realization strikes that career advancement takes a combination of uncommon abilities and indispensable connections.

You can't live with politics,
and
you can't live without them

The person who can frame the issues and shape the discussion regarding career advancement stands a better chance of coming out ahead.

Example _____

As a you-can-do-it framework for analyzing career politics, the text can be used to assess risks and navigate one's career by discussing the pros and cons of various career perspectives. Ultimately, the application of any career maneuvers and ethics is a matter of individual style and personal choice. It is important to understand the forces that forge a person's career and not to be caught off balance. Successful executives will tell you to never give up and never be under prepared. In the end, the bottom line as it relates to profit making, productivity, and employee morale benefits from a candid discussion about the politics of promotion. When there is straight talk about career advancement, people can make better long-and short-range career decisions.

A prudent question is one-half of wisdom. Francis Bacon

Achieving the clarity needed to resolve promotion paradoxes requires an awareness of the dynamics of career advancement. Career advancement dynamics should not be mistaken for career counseling, which involves aptitude testing and prepares people for the labor pool. As good as career counseling is, it does not always translate into advancement to the executive level. This is certainly true in today's competitive workplace, which requires an aggressive stance in the way that promotions are planned and pursued.

Promotion Politics are too important not to be discussed.
Especially, if higher-ups are secretly grooming you for a top job over other qualified staff.

If one benefits from this and keeps quiet, is this behavior

Ethical ____ Unethical ____ Gray (neither one) ____

Explain_____

Actually, people have various ways of discussing career politics. However, a lot of the discussion seems to be emotionally charged and lacks a well thought out philosophical base. Negative comments tend to be counterproductive and fail to make the breakthroughs needed to change promotion practices. Possessing the will to talk about career advancement politics can be life-altering as people learn about themselves and what makes the organization tick. People seeking career advancement should have insights that motivate them to map out and discuss the pros and cons of the promotion practices. In order to pursue career advancement as it is played out in the workplace, people must be prepared to accept that upward mobility may require a person to sometimes think like an impersonal institution and to sometimes think like a sensitive, caring person.

*Why can't somebody give us a list of things that everybody thinks
and nobody says, another list of things that everybody says and
nobody thinks?*   *Oliver Wendell Holmes*

For example, some people have been told that preselection,
preferential treatment, and politics do not exist in today's modern
enlightened organizations. They also have been led to believe that
people who tend to manipulate others or subtly seek out special
treatment probably have a moral weakness and are somehow not
worthy of promotion. In actuality, politics exists and needs to be
dealt with in a highly professional and business manner.

The Voice of Reason

**When people learn to speak the language of
career advancement it gives them
new vistas and new terminology.**

**This improves their ability to discuss career-molding
issues with a focus on what can make them more
successful.**

There is more to be gained by approaching career politics in a
forthright manner than by minimizing or denying the role it plays
in advancement. The decision as to what to conceal and what to
reveal makes the politics of promotion an intriguing study of human
nature. This is so true because the politics of promotion contains all
the wisdom and foolishness found in the workplace.

Warts and All

**The ugly truth about career advancement politics
is found in those things that are kept hushed up.**

Lorenzo Flores

Real World Model for Career Advancement: Promotion Paradoxes

The ability to learn faster than your competitors may be the only sustainable competitive advantage.

Arie P. de Geus

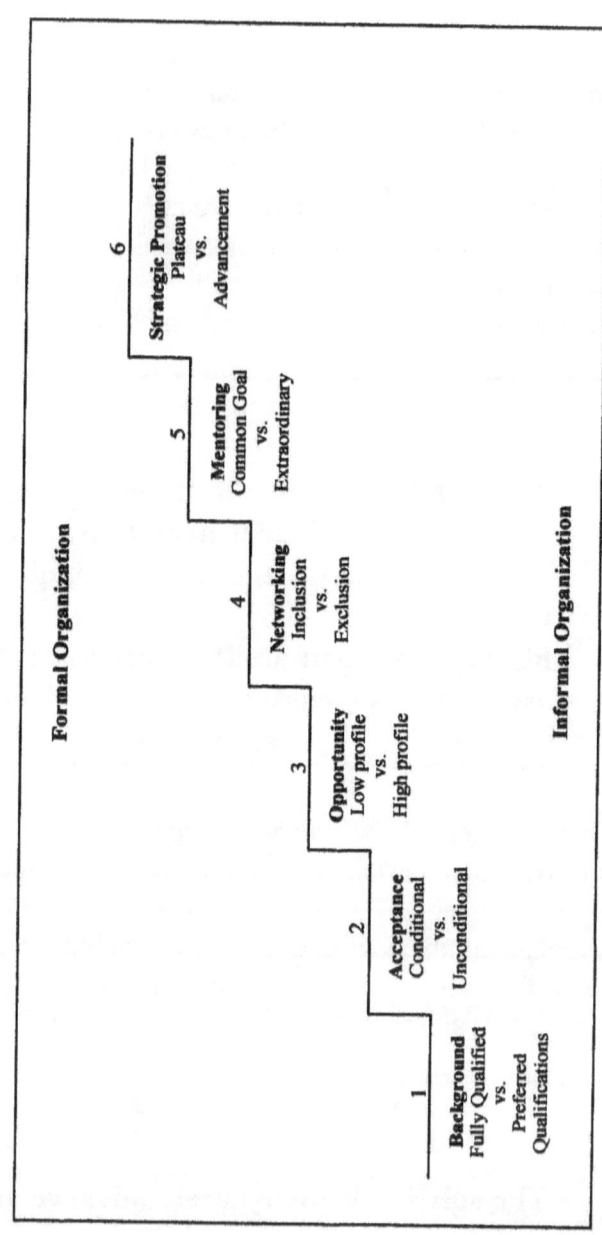

Formal Organization

1
Background
Fully Qualified
vs.
Preferred
Qualifications

2
Acceptance
Conditional
vs.
Unconditional

3
Opportunity
Low profile
vs.
High profile

4
Networking
Inclusion
vs.
Exclusion

5
Mentoring
Common Goal
vs.
Extraordinary

6
Strategic Promotion
Plateau
vs.
Advancement

Informal Organization

Career Shaping Questions

1. **Political Savoir Faire. How astute are you in handling reciprocity, contingency plans, influencing strategies, flanking movements, negotiations, compromise maneuvers, and diversionary tactics?**

   Circle your choice.

   1   2   3   4   5   6   7   8   9   10
   I have   **I have**
   entry-level   **CEO-level**
   skills   **skills**

   Explain: _____

2. **Performing at a higher level. Every career promotion requires you to develop new formal and informal skill sets.**

   Mark your choice. Yes____   No____

   Explain: _____

3. **What is told to new hires about the organization's promotion process? What concepts and ideas does management use to explain how people are promoted?**

   Explain: _____

4. **Why is it that many executives don't tell employees about the political realities of career advancement?**

   Explain: _____

Background Qualifications

Fully Qualified vs. Preferred Qualifications

No man's knowledge goes beyond his experience. John Locke

Many people are under the impression that management is always on the lookout for talented, educated, and ambitious people to move up the career ladder. While this may be the spoken message, a lot of circumstantial factors come into play. Depending on management's inclinations and the applicant's

> appearance
> credentials
> social heritage
> potential
> and work experience,

a person's rate of advancement can be slowed or accelerated. Not surprisingly, it all turns on how management interprets the candidate's background in light of what it feels is the ideal candidate's background.

Calling the Shots Is a Heady Feeling

The ability to rate and rank a candidate's experience and potential is a management tool by which people are promoted or eliminated as competitors. It is based on issues of substance or artificial contrivances.

In career advancement, issues of substance may refer to a lack of professional credentials. Artificial contrivances pertain to purely subjective impressions about people. For example, a person may not be hired or promoted because he or she consciously or subconsciously reminds the boss of a rival. In this sense, any "fair or foul" method might be used to determine who is fully qualified and who has the preferred qualifications.

Background Qualifications: Fully Qualified

If you want to get along, go along. Sam Rayburn

Fully qualified means that the candidate has the requisite technical skills and human relations skills needed for the position. These primary traits suggest that the person can handle the assigned duties and responsibilities.

Power Broker to the Underdog

Most people applying for a position have the basic skills to become a topnotch employee. What they are lacking is an opportunity from someone who is willing to take a risk on them.

Being ranked as fully qualified means passing the first round of evaluations. Listed below are the formal metrics used to measure whether a person has met the prerequisites for a position.

Formal Metrics

Requirements	Measurable Factors
Education	Diplomas, licenses, and certificates
Experience	A period of formal training/work record
Accomplishments	Quantifiable achievements/contributions
Physical Requirements	Eyesight, hearing, lifting ability
Age	Prevailing practice and needs
Performance Evaluations	Meets expectations for the position
References	People who can vouch for someone's productivity and efficiency

Preferred Qualifications

Power politics is the diplomatic name for the law of the jungle.
Ely Culbertson

Whether searching for the exceptional employee or the candidate of their fantasies, managers rely on their unspoken privileges in making a placement decision. By exercising his or her personal prerogatives, an executive sets the cultural climate that influences the organization in terms of tolerance for certain types of people, work styles, and ideas. In effect, executives have a political license that allows them to bestow favors and promote people. Also, executive titles come with built-in immunity from certain things that are said and done. Thus the X Factor is alive and well and living in the boss's entitlements, indulgences, liberties, and the powers to do as he or she sees fit in the name of doing what is best for the organization. Sometimes this can make executives appear to be immune from accountability and above the laws that govern mere mortals.

Power Player Is as Power Player Does

Power Hungry
Power Breakfast
Power Lunch
Power Moves
Power Grab

Sometimes at the core of executive privileges are willful prejudices, disguised as objective decision making. They are used to rationalize why some people are promoted and others are not.

The X Factor, which is embodied in the boss's prerogatives, enables the boss to look beyond a person's marketable skills and study the added value that he or she brings to the bargaining table. The freedom to make personal choices is justified as a means of finding people who are a "seamless fit" with the organization.

Preferred Qualifications

Politics can be good or bad.
Few things get done without a power base.
Hence, many of our finest managers are closet politicians...Those
that make things happen are politically skilled and understand
the use of power.
Robert H. Waterman

What Have You Done for Me Lately?

Many times, in the name of team work or organizational development, executives favor someone for promotion who will advance their self-interest, which is a mixture of business, political, and personal needs.

True _____False _____ Other _____

Explain _____

By using their executive prerogatives, higher-ups control who is allowed into the "talent pipeline," which leads to key positions. For example, an executive may rationalize or cloak his or her hiring of a close friend by stating:

He or she complements my skills
or
He or she compensates for my weaknesses

In the end, it comes down to protecting oneself and asking some pretty selfish questions that go to the heart of loyalty to the boss.

* How comfortable am I with this person?
* Can I trust him or her with the truth, power, and information?
* How well does this person follow orders?
* Will this person take the blame for mistakes?

Preferred Qualifications: Unofficial Secondary Traits

Once the people begin to reason, all is lost. Voltaire

In determining how people are hired and promoted, it is important to study the primary objective qualifications and the secondary subjective qualifications (p. 39). Often times the subjective factors outnumber the objective factors. Even so, people are told that promotions are based on unbiased criteria. This gives rise to "social promotions," which are based on both skill level and how well a person fits into the boss's discriminating comfort zone.

It's All Relative To How The Boss Sees The World

The comfort zone is the sum total of the primary and secondary traits that add up to how well the boss can relate to you.

The comfort zone is so subjective that it provides a great deal of latitude in making decisions. It encompasses personal, psychological, and social-political factors that make one person feel at ease with another person. From the boss's perspective the inherent question is "How much does he or she remind me of myself?" Thus, informalities and spontaneous feelings impact the way one is perceived and how one relates to co-workers. Unless a person fits into management's comfort zone, he or she is seen as challenging the comfort zone, which may be threatening to the boss.

The Paradox Of Background Qualifications
Nothing succeeds like the appearance of success. Christopher Lasch

The candidate must have the right qualifications that enable him or her to simultaneously meet management's subjective and objective criteria.

Promotion By Comfort Zone
Primary Traits and Secondary Traits

Official Primary Traits (Things that are valued)	**Unofficial Secondary Traits** (Things that bring added value)
Education	**Education**
Possession of license, diploma, certificate, college degree(s).	What college did you go to? Are you a family legacy to an Ivy League University? Type of degree, license, diploma.
Experience	**Special Personal Contacts**
Training received and positions held. Customary letters of reference.	Who do you know and who knows you? What does your spouse do? Who does he or she know? How handy will these contacts be?
Physical requirements	**Physical Appearance and Language**
Eyesight, hearing, lifting.	Race, gender, height, weight, disability, light vs. dark complexion. Lifestyle preferences. Attractiveness rating may range from movie star looks to frumpy. Is speech accent considered wonderful or appalling?
Age	**Social, Political, Economic History**
18 years old or not more than 70 years old.	Political party, military service, sports, religion. Written record of ancestry bloodlines. Upbringing: lower-middle-or upper-class pedigree.
Accomplishments	**Accomplishments**
Achievements and contributions.	Extra assignments and special positions created for professional development.

Primary Traits are Door Openers,
but
Secondary Traits are Destiny

Trahey's Simple Rule: Would you hire you?

People who overcome personal adversity learn to develop their primary traits and augment them with as many secondary traits as possible. Individuals born into wealth and privilege have a jump start over other people, but they must also have the basic skills. Plus they are aware that they need the polish and finishing touches provided by the secondary traits. In either case, to thrive and survive, people must appreciate the dynamic interplay between the primary and secondary traits. Sometimes the secondary traits carry as much weight (or more) as the primary traits. They may pick up where the primary traits leave off and tip the scale in favor of a particular candidate.

List Your Primary Traits

_____   _____   _____

List Your Secondary Traits

_____   _____   _____

Given that few people openly talk about the primary and secondary traits or how closed minded they are towards other people, the comfort zone tends to operate at a subconscious preselection level. Due to the seductive power of the comfort zone, a mental shift may occur in the boss's thinking process as he or she ponders how to best use a person. This may happen when the boss weighs what the candidate brings to the table and compares it to what he or she desires or needs on a personal or professional level.

Career Shaping Questions

1. **Write in the steps you would take to deal with the Paradox of Background Qualifications, which states: Simultaneously you must have the right subjective and objective qualifications that please the higher-ups.**

    _____

    _____

    _____

2. **Assess the pros and cons of this Career Advancement Paradox.**

Pros	Cons
_____	_____
_____	_____

3. **To succeed in your organization what did you have to unlearn about career advancement and what new things did you have to learn about career advancement politics?**

    Explain _____

4. **"Life is what you make of it"**

    How does this statement square with the reality that you must please your higher-ups to get promoted or maintain your position.

    Explain _____

Career Shaping Questions

5. **How have higher-ups or your peers dealt with the Paradox of Background Qualifications? Give specific examples.**

    _____

6. **List factors that make up your personal and professional comfort zone.**

    _____

7. **List factors that comprise the boss's personal and professional comfort zone.**

    _____

8. **List similarities (See questions 6 and 7 above) between your comfort zone and the boss's comfort zone.**

    Boss's comfort zone   **My comfort zone**

    _____   _____

    _____   _____

    _____   _____

Career Shaping Questions

9. **Write a plan that will help you work with the boss's comfort zone.**

    Step 1 _____

    Step 2 _____

    Step 3 _____

10. **How can management intentionally create career advancement politics and rivalries between co-workers?**

    _____

11. **How can management unintentionally create career advancement politics and rivalries between co-workers?**

    _____

12. **To what degree do you feel your boss uses politics (hard work blended with appearances, emotions, and words) to get him or herself promoted or to maintain their position?**

    1   2   3   4   5   6   7   8   9   10
    Never   Always

    Explain _____

13. **To what degree do you use politics (hard work blended with appearances, emotions, and words) to get promoted or to maintain your position?**

    1   2   3   4   5   6   7   8   9   10
    Never   Always

    Explain _____

Acceptance

Conditional vs. Unconditional

The deepest principle in human nature is the craving to be appreciated.
William James

Are people held in high esteem or low esteem by the boss and co-workers? How much backing do they receive from the people they work with? In many ways, the workplace is like high school all over again, with cliques and popularity contests, which take various forms in the work environment. These adolescent forms of behavior should never be factors in career advancement, but it's part of our calculating human nature to like one person more than another. Therefore, workplace relationships take on a new level of importance as people decide what political and social circles they want to "hang out with."

A Friend:
Someone who knows your shortcomings
and still likes you

**Peer group approval is a prerequisite for
career progress.**

At work are there work teams or work cliques? Do the work teams give acceptance to all co-workers? These questions arise as workers and executives seek out people they feel at ease with. Acceptance requires the formation of a mainly unspoken social contract of support with one's work group, e.g., superiors, subordinates, and community contacts. The dynamics of acceptance in the workplace includes the conditional and unconditional factors that will be discussed in the following pages. Both the conditional and unconditional factors have a strong bearing on an individual's morale, ethics, and productivity. The heart of the acceptance structure is the work group's power to give someone a warm welcome and ongoing career support. Or to let a person's career languish by giving him or her lukewarm approval - the equivalent of sabotaging a person's career.

Conditional Acceptance

Conditional vs. Unconditional

Whom the gods wish to destroy they first call promising. C. Connolly

Yes, you are a good worker, but we are not sure this organization is the right place for you. The word but negates everything that went before it. Conditional acceptance is marked by limited approval ratings from peers and superiors. People may receive a very tepid welcome or just enough support to keep them placated, but not enough to advance them. Somehow, they are perceived as not quite ready for advancement. Typically, statements showing conditional acceptance are expressed in the following ways:

- **He or she hasn't been here long enough.**
- **He or she doesn't have the right work ethic. Needs training.**
- **His or her background is different from the rest of the group.**
- **His or her work never quite lives up to expectations.**

When people have unselfishly done all that they have been told to do and still don't receive support for promotion, their inability to move ahead can be traced back to the limitations placed on them by the dominant controlling group.

Halo or Horns

Depending on the degree of "favorable opinion" a person receives from his or her co-workers, he or she may be invited or left out of the information loop.

People perceived as outsiders cannot compete with members of the insider groups. Without a sense of belonging, the alternative is resentment and/or inferiority feelings when it comes to advancement. Making someone feel like an outsider or impostor is a tactic used by insecure people who want to derail a person's career or make themselves feel superior. The key to finding acceptance lies in the quality and quantity of positive interactions one has with peers and higher ups.

Unconditional Acceptance

Conditional vs. Unconditional

The more one knows about a person,
the greater one's power to destroy him. Stanley I. Benn

The best affirmation that can be received from one's peers is to be able to compete with them on an equal footing. A person accepted unconditionally receives full approval, the equivalent of a "crazy about you" kind of embrace from co-workers. The person is seen as an integral part of the work team and regarded by peers as a leader in training who reflects the organization's high standards.

Plays Well With Others?

(at office politics)
Circle your choice

No, I do not   1   2   3   4   5   6   7   8   9   10   **Yes, I do**

Explain _____

Not surprisingly, the individual accepted unconditionally (the Golden Boy or Girl) benefits from the social similarities that he has in common with the dominant controlling group. This friendly type of alliance building may be based on age, class, race, education or gender. Chumming up to the boss may involve joining community organizations or private clubs in which he or she is a member. In some cases this may be a means of group bonding, but it may also be a means of discriminating against certain classes and types of people.

Paradox Of Acceptance

People are always ready to admit a man's ability after he gets there.
Bob Edwards

On a personal level, always be yourself, don't try to be something you're not. However, for professional validation and to win management's confidence, you must blend in with its social, economic, and political leanings.

Acceptance:
An Essential Management Tool

Conditional vs. Unconditional

Though this be madness, yet there is method in it.
William Shakespeare

It seems that the ratio, rate, and combination of factors that determine the degree to which one is accepted into a group fall into two categories. One is personal traits and the other is professional traits. The only difference between the two is the subjective thinking of the decision maker, who must decide whom to promote and why. Below are some of the factors that tend to influence the hiring and promotion process.

Promotion Metrics

Personal Metrics	Professional Metrics
Age	Associates and acquaintances
Accent	Bottom-line oriented
Ethnicity	Credentials
Family background	Customer service oriented
Gender	Education
Health history	Knowledge of the job
Height	Leadership
Lifestyle	Loyalty
Marital status	Management skills
Military experience	Negotiation skills
Physical attractiveness	Peer group relations
Physical disability	Potential
Primary language	Problem solving
Race	Profit and loss management
Religion	Professional demeanor
Secondary language	Quality of work
Sexual preference	Reciprocity minded
Social class	Seniority
Temperament	Teamwork
Weight	Technical expertise

Career Shaping Questions

1. **Write in the steps you would take to deal with the Career Advancement Paradox of Acceptance which states:**

   On a personal level, always be your authentic self; e.g., don't try to be something you're not. However, for professional validation and to win management's confidence, you must blend in with its social, economic, and political leanings.

   _____   _____

   _____   _____

2. **Analyze the pros and cons of this Career Advancement Paradox?**

Pros	Cons
_____	_____
_____	_____

3. **How are new employees shown acceptance by higher-ups?**

   Explain _____

4. **How are new employees shown acceptance by their peers?**

   Explain _____

Career Shaping Questions

5. **How have higher-ups or your peers dealt with the Career Advancement Paradox of Acceptance?**

    Explain _____

6. **How do you rate your quality (degree of excellence) of interaction with your immediate boss?**

    Circle your choice.
    1   2   3   4   5   6   7   8   9   10
    No   Extremely
    interaction   interactive

    Explain _____

7. **How do you rate your quality (degree of excellence) of interaction with higher ups - top management?**

    Circle your choice.
    1   2   3   4   5   6   7   8   9   10
    No   Extremely
    interaction   interactive

    Explain _____

8. **To what degree are there cliques* masquerading as work teams in your workplace?**

    Circle your choice.
    1   2   3   4   5   6   7   8   9   10
    None   Extensive

    Explain _____

*groups of people who seldom mingle with those outside their inner circle of close friends.

Career Shaping Questions

9. At work some people state:

1. I avoid politics, I just do my job.
2. We don't play political games in this organization.
3. I don't kiss up to anyone.
4. Career advancement politics do not apply to my position because _____

(fill in the blank)

Scrutinize the above statements by asking the following questions which reflect workplace politics.

Circle your choice - Yes or No

A. Do you laugh at your boss's wit and humor?	Yes No
B. Do you wish people happy birthday, holidays?	Yes No
C. Do you get to work on time?	Yes No
D. Do you volunteer for extra work?	Yes No
E. Do you dress appropriately for work?	Yes No
F. Do you plan ahead in order to keep your job?	Yes No
G. Do you plan to get promoted?	Yes No
H. Do you meet deadlines set by your boss?	Yes No
I. Do you watch what you say at work?	Yes No
J. Do you stay on everyone's good side?	Yes No

If you answered yes to any of the above questions - you politic at work, but you may not recognize it. However, your co-workers do. Career maintenance or career advancement requires you to develop your own brand of politicking and realize that everything has a political twist which generates favorable or unfavorable reactions. Doing what it takes to maintain or advance your position requires numerous daily acts of political vanity and political humility.

The Opportunity Structure

Low Profile vs. High Profile

There are people who interview extremely well and perform poorly, but the reverse is also true. There are lots of people who interview terribly, but have done a great job.   *Paul W. Barada*

Organizations are proud to say that they like problem solvers. And, they are quick to add that creative people know that problems are actually opportunities in disguise. The art of being a problem solver entails the skill of knowing how to position oneself to receive opportunities to solve problems, which brings maximum rewards and recognition. Becoming the "go-to-guy" or "go-to-gal" for problem solving is a two-way street.

Everyday Is a Political Aptitude Test

Management knows what the issues and problems are. The potential problem solver must, in some way, impress management that he or she is the best person to fix the problem.

Organizations know that not all problem solving opportunities are equal. Shrewd executives sort out the minor from the major problems and decide which person will receive the high status assignment and who will get the low status assignment. Or, as some executives like to describe it, "giving someone the opportunity to show his stuff and shine." The problem list may go from simple "fix it" issues to profound organizational changes. Thus, for the most part, higher-ups control the process of doling out opportunities. And, they are picky about the type of problem solvers they select and how the assignment will affect their career advancement. They want someone who will make them look good and bring a great return on their investment of time.

The Opportunity Structure

Low Profile vs. High Profile

The Golden Rule. He who has the gold makes the rules.
Anonymous

An ambitious person can on his or her own try to develop a reputation for problem solving by going in search of the right opportunities to work on. Although this independent course of action is admirable, it is highly unlikely to result in major progress for a person who is not in someway politically connected to management. Don't let anyone tell you that connections don't count. The problem with problem solving is not having the opportunity to solve problems, but being selected to solve the right problems that bring the right exposure to upper management. The more connections people have, the more options and protection they have in the workplace. You can never have too many options or protectors.

TOP
Timing, Opportunity, Planning

Precious career advancement time can be lost unless a person is in a position to know what management considers to be low profile or high profile problem solving.

For want of direction and proper guidance, a person can be left running in place or spinning his or her wheels and not getting the right breaks needed to move up the career ladder. Other ambitious people may position themselves so that higher-ups who have political pull can begin to "bring them along." Higher-ups may assign problem solving tasks that are appropriate to a trainee or protege's skill level. The tasks increase in complexity and rewards as the individual shows that he or she has passed the test of trust as defined by higher-ups. Trust must always be earned on a daily basis by using good taste in the way you express fealty and confidence in the boss's leadership.

The Opportunity Structure

(Continued)

Low Profile vs. High Profile

As organizational researchers, we have wondered why certain decisions are made and particular strategies chosen. Why does an organization end up with a particular kind of structure? Why is a certain individual selected for a particular job?...[T]he problems of many troubled companies are deeply ingrained, based on the deep seated neurotic styles and fantasies of top executives.

Manfred F.R. Kets de Vries and Danny Miller

Executive Quirks

Selfish ego involvement to some degree is present in every boss's decision-making process. Choosing what tasks to assign, and to whom, is a peculiar mixture of professional interest and personal tricks of behavior.

What idiosyncratic actions does your boss go through before taking action?

Example _____

This crazy like a fox behavior is aimed at making things look different from what they are. It exemplifies how higher-ups keep people clueless by distracting them. This practice allows executives to get things by people without their noticing it. Analyzing and being alert to these ploys can elevate your career advancement acumen. The opportunity structure determines the extent to which management is willing to invest in a person. To better comprehend it, the next section examines it from the perspective of what differentiates a low profile opportunity from a high profile opportunity.

Low Profile Opportunity

Low Profile vs. High Profile

Ability is of little account without opportunity. Napoleon Bonaparte

For the most part, management controls the timing, the degree of personal involvement, and the level of exposure to higher-ups that a person is given.

To Advance, the Average Person Must Stand Out And Fit In

Within reason, potential problem solvers should look for ways to connect with higher-ups and leave them feeling good about knowing you.

Example _____

Only the managerial elite know the true significance of opportunities and are positioned to assign them as they see appropriate. Unfortunately, many people with high potential are given low-level assignments, which bring little or no exposure to top management. Successfully completing low profile opportunities should be the ideal way to gain experience. After having proved one's mettle, one should be allowed to progress to higher level assignments, which attract the attention of higher-ups. This is not always the case, as higher-ups are in a position to influence subordinates into taking lower level opportunities. Subordinates may be enticed by such statements as "this opportunity has great potential," when it actually has none or only limited possibilities for advancing a person's career. This type of beguilement may result in strong feelings of resentment against management, which can spread to other staff members.

Low Profile Opportunity

Low Profile vs. High Profile

If you wish in this world to advance
Your merits you're bound to enhance
You must stir it and stump it
And blow your own trumpet,
Or trust me, you haven't a chance
W.S. Gilbert

Potential problem solvers should be aware that the opportunity structure is a political management tool that can be used to sidetrack and dissuade certain people from pursuing higher opportunities. A steady diet of low impact assignments, generally, means that a person is working steadily to retain his or her position. However, he or she is not receiving opportunities that will nourish and accelerate his or her career.

Life Is About Keeping Your Options Open

Receiving training in technical skills is great, but this is geared towards making people well-disciplined followers.

On the other hand, receiving management skills training and extraordinary mentoring are designed to develop future leaders.

One pattern of low profile opportunities is training, which prepares people to be good contributors and technicians. Depending on your needs, you may choose whether to follow this track or seek other avenues for success. There is nothing wrong with being a technician or follower as long as you are aware of the pros and cons of your decision.

High Profile Opportunity

Low Profile vs. High Profile

I have climbed to the top of a greasy pole. Benjamin Disraeli

In career advancement, high profile refers to assignments that result in extensive contact with the organization's power brokers. Generally, high impact opportunities that enable a person to demonstrate his or her talents are planned to some degree by extraordinary mentors, who advocate for the person's career development.

Gentlemen's Agreement

In preparing people for key positions, little is left to happenstance. High profile opportunities are special stretch assignments that enable people to extend their range of technical knowledge and professional expertise.

The combined leverage of having the right opportunities and mentoring has a high impact on a person's upward mobility into management positions, where special skills sets are needed. At another level, random or accidental occurrences, which are very rare, can sometimes provide people with a chance to show their abilities. Often times, the secrets to Career Advancement lie hidden in the organization's opportunity structure, which is controlled by the managerial elitist. This is clearly evidenced when managers give a high profile opportunity to their "handpicked" favorite person and then work to make it look like a low profile opportunity. This is tantamount to a conspiracy in which managers must be in accord and keep things quiet. Repercussions could be bad for the person who leaks information to the staff about what is really going on. In referring to this traitotous behavior some executives make the gibing remark that "no good deed goes unpunished." Intrinsic in the Executive Code of Silence are phrases like: Don't buck the system, don't rock the boat, and don't make waves.

High Profile Opportunity

Real politics are the possession and distribution of power. B. Disraeli

Making a high profile opportunity look like a low profile opportunity requires political polish and good taste in the selection of words. Some leaders string their words together so that they are circumspect, yet seemingly informative when they speak. This requires the speaker to use soothing words that tranquilize the audience into believing what is said.

Just Finesse It

Have the grace and wit to handle difficult situations skillfully and diplomatically.

The speaker may use guile and contrivances to persuade people to his or her point of view. Telltale signs of finesse occur when the speaker gingerly plays down or minimizes hot issues. Statements are engineered to carefully avoid answering direct questions. Asking thought provoking questions tends to be discouraged. Making high profile opportunities appear like low profile opportunities is one of the keys to career advancement. This may involve schemes, which mislead staff and outsiders into thinking that promotion opportunities are fairly distributed. Eventually, management's real intentions subtly make themselves known. Consequently, management may lose credibility because the staff sees the cloaked moves for what they are--manipulating people by playing favorites and playing games.

The Dual Paradoxes Of Opportunity

1. All at the same time, welcome low profile opportunities, but proactively pursue high profile opportunities that create advantages.

2. Learn how to disguise high profile opportunities as low profile opportunities.

Opportunity Structure:
A Key Management Tool

A man is not always what he appears to be, but what he appears to be is always a significant part of what he is. Willard Gaylin

When all the resumes look alike, all it takes is one tie-breaking experience to move ahead. In some cases, the tie-breaker may have been set up by management to give a particular person an advantage. Management can do this by making high profile advantages appear very low profile. Listed below are some low and high profile opportunities that allow one to compare and contrast the differences that give some people the competitive edge.

Low Profile Opportunity (Training to be a follower)	**High Profile Opportunity** (Training to be a leader)
General computer training	Special computer skills for one of a kind projects
Telephone etiquette	Custom designed stretch assignments
Customer service skills	Management training
General staff development	Leadership skills
Presentations at staff meetings	Presentations to higher-up executives
Staff potluck lunch	Going with the boss to his or her favorite restaurant
Occasionally filling in for supervisor	Organization subsidizes a person's advanced university degree

Assessing The Potential Of An Assignment

If ambition doesn't hurt you, you haven't got it. K. Norris

Does it pass the smell test? Use your political instincts to analyze the value of opportunities. The trick is to know how much potential an assignment has. Don't assume anything. For the sake of your career it is important to ensure that you are being set up for success and not set up for failure or to be marginalized. Before committing oneself, it is necessary to ask about the who, what, when, where, why, and how of the task. To some people these are inconvenient questions. By finding answers to these thorny issues you will stay ahead of the power curve and make better career decisions.

Who

Make time to meet the people in the chain of command. Identify the key person(s) you will be reporting to. Know the power broker who has the final say in approving your work and ideas.

What

Understand as much as possible about management's agenda, as well as the parameters and the history of the assignment. Consider the pros and cons of the assignment. Heed any ethical issues and unintended consequences.

When

Time frame – start date and end date of the assignment? Once the task has started are there any potential problems or surprises to be aware of?

Where

Location of the assignment. Are you willing to travel or relocate? Where will sources of personal and professional support be available?

Why

Identify the formal and informal reasons you were selected? Why this assignment and why now? Ascertain reasons other people turned it down or were never offered the assignment.

How

Note the process and all the steps necessary to finish the project. How will completion of the assignment benefit the organization, your career, and the careers of the people up the hierarchy chain?

Career Shaping Questions

1. **Write steps to deal with the Career Advancement Dual Paradoxes of Opportunity, which states:**

   A. **Welcome low profile opportunities, but proactively pursue high profile opportunities that create advantages.**

   B. **Learn how to disguise high profile opportunities as low profile opportunities. Thus, a person can achieve his or her promotion agenda without others noticing what is actually occurring.**

   _____   _____

   _____   _____

2. **What are the pros and cons of this Career Advancement Dual Paradox?**

   Pros   **Cons**

   _____   _____

   _____   _____

Career Shaping Questions

3. How have higher-ups or co-workers dealt with the Career Advancement Dual Paradoxes of Opportunity?

_____

4. Describe the concepts of:

High profile opportunity _____

Low profile opportunity _____

5. List the most sought after high status assignments, projects, tasks, or appointments in your organization (unit, department). These are the types that provide you with quality "face time" with higher-ups.

_____   _____   _____

_____   _____   _____

_____   _____   _____

Career Shaping Questions

6. **How are people chosen for high visibility assignments or projects?**

   Explain _____

7. **In your career, how many high profile opportunities (preparing you for promotions) have you received? Write in the number** _____

   Example _____

8. **What stories does your boss tell about the way that he or she advanced up the career ladder?**

   Explain _____

9. **What are your personal Career Advancement stories - what you did or did not do to get promoted?**

   Explain _____

Career Shaping Questions

10. **The boss is your entree to higher positions. How much are you willing to flatter him or her in order to secure a high visibility opportunity?**

    Circle your choice.

1	2	3	4	5	6	7	8	9	10

    **I never
    butter up
    the boss**   **I always praise
    and compliment
    the boss**

    Explain _____

11. **If you have received a high profile opportunity, what formal and informal steps did you take to position yourself in order to obtain that opportunity?**

    **List formal steps
    (On the record)**

    _____   _____

    _____   _____

    **List informal steps
    (Off the record)**

    _____   _____

    _____   _____

Networking

Inclusion vs. Exclusion

*Friendship is an arrangement by which we
undertake to exchange small favors for big ones.*
Baron de Montesquieu

Nothing gets more attention than beginning a conversation with the phrase, "My sources tell me." This brings to light the "Off-the-Record Club," which is an informal pipeline that controls information and leaks rumors. Since the beginning of time, networking has been used to plant information, disseminate facts, gather intelligence, and seek new information. In some situations it has led to the creation of a "network of spies" that is used to keep tabs on the competition. The fact is, we are dependent on others for revealing information that can be used to either help people or exploit opportunities to one's advantage.

The Off-the-Record Club

**People who have mastered the network know
that networking can take a generic form, where
everyone is included, or it can take an elitist form,
where certain people are excluded from participation.**

In spite of its sometimes questionable role and functions, workplace networking seems to be presented as a wholesome, career enriching process. It refers to the active participation in the "give and take" of the communication systems that exist inside and outside an organization. What better way to make connections, generate business, and get tips for career advancement? This is why it is imperative to understand the exact nature of the network structure that exists in the organization and how it is used in an inclusive or exclusive way. The boss and co-workers may treat a person in one of three ways: embrace, keep at arm's length, or reject entirely.

Networking
by
Inclusion

Inclusion vs. Exclusion

Any time friends have to be careful of what they say to friends, friendship is taking another dimension. Duke Ellington

Regardless of a person's background, the inclusion level of group interaction is open to everyone. Networking is strongly encouraged by organization higher-ups as a way of cultivating contacts. The valuable associations that you make are only as good as the followup that goes into nurturing and maintaining these relationships for future use.

Pressing the Flesh, Pumping the Arm
and Bending the Elbow

**As a basic "get to know people" approach,
social networking is a good way to trade ideas and
exchange business cards.**

I play the game for the game's sake.
Sherlock Holmes

As helpful as networking is, its main drawback is that the quantity and quality of information available is limited to the number of higher-ups who attend the networking meeting. And the higher-ups' willingness to disclose what actually goes into the executive promotion process. In other words, if everyone at the networking session is at the worker bee level, the information sharing is not the same as if the Queen Bee was participating in the cross pollination of information.

Networking By Exclusion

Inclusion vs. Exclusion

People seem to enjoy things more when they know a lot of other
people have been left out of the pleasure.   Russell Baker

As someone once astutely said, "The only reason for adults to give a party is to not invite certain people." This seems to apply to networking by exclusion, which refers to gatherings where admission is by "invitation only." Metaphorically speaking, making the preferred **A** list is better than being on the **B** list of people who are invited only when **A**-list people cannot attend. **C** list people rarely get invited. People often compete for these coveted invitations to evening parties and receptions because they form the basis for high-level information sharing. Even when it's understood that no business is allowed to be discussed, private clubs and swank social parties allow people to "mix and mingle" with people in positions of high status. These can appear to be merely fortuitous meetings, but in reality they may be well planned in advance, rehearsed for effect, and measured for timing.

Eat My Dust

Since there are no rules governing these exclusive cliques, they are the perfect tools for meeting people in neutral settings and excluding unwanted persons from key decisions.

Cavorting in these soirees is not seen as excluding people or as discrimination. To the contrary, working the room like a politician and "hobnobbing" is characterized as spending quality time with peers. A lot of future business is riding on these social gatherings and cocktail talk. If "deal cutting" occurs, it is instantly redefined as socializing and making casual acquaintances for future endeavors. Surely, to see and to be seen in the company of organization royalty increases one's personal stock.

Networking By Exclusion

The word politics comes from the Greek: Poli, meaning many,
and tics meaning bloodsuckers.   *George Stephanopoulos*

It might be said that a person who can do all of the aforementioned has mastered the social graces of smooth talking, adulation of higher-ups, and working with the common folk. Very likely, his or her aspirations and personality mesh well with those of the group he or she is seeking to bond with. Once a person is a member of the in-group, nothing can match the thrill and adrenalin rush of power networking one's way to the top.

Carousing for Fun and Profit

Networkers allow themselves to be used by people and in return they know how to use people to achieve their goals.

Using and being used is the basis for reciprocity, which is the possession of a mindset that encourages people to trade favors in the name of helping one another. This is the way relationships are maintained among the individuals and groups that are involved in networking by exclusion. The players understand the mix of business, hard work, and sometimes twisted egos. Given their ambitious drive and hunger for success, they are able to gain political traction by embracing the whole formal and informal process, which includes diligent work, gift giving, and doing favors for associates.

Paradox Of Networking

Love thy neighbor as thyself, but choose your neighborhood.
Louise Beal

Networking your way to success requires sharing information with others. But, you must reserve the most prized knowledge and contacts for personal advantage.

Network System:
The Difference Between
Inclusion And Exclusion

Have the daring to accept yourself as a bundle of possibilities
and undertake the game of making the most of your best.
H. E. Fosdick

People who want to advance must know the difference between the two networking systems and position themselves to use both. While one is open to everyone, the other requires close personal and professional relationships with the who's who of the organization.

Networking by Inclusion (Everyone participates)	**Networking by Exclusion** (The chosen few)
Presentation at employee's brown paper bag lunch - emphasis on building technical skills	Power lunch with the higher ups - emphasis on acquiring leadership skills and techniques
Employee picnic at public park	Barbecue at boss's private beach house or hunting lodge
Staff retreat	Retreat for management only
Membership in professional organizations, emphasis on skill building	Membership in exclusive clubs, warm convivialities for personal growth and advancement
Casual employee activities, birthdays and holiday parties for everyone's enjoyment	Being selected for the boss's special team empowers people to participate in office activities and meetings "off limits" to persons not in the "insiders group."

Career Shaping Questions

1. **Write steps to deal with the Career Advancement Paradox of Networking, which states:**

   Networking your way to success requires sharing information with others but reserving the most prized knowledge and contacts for personal advantage.

   _____

   _____

2. **Identify the pros and cons of this Career Advancement Paradox.**

Pros	Cons
_____	_____
_____	_____
_____	_____

Career Shaping Questions

3. **How have higher-ups or your peers dealt with the Career Advancement Paradox of Opportunity?**

   Explain _____

4. **In terms of moving you up to the executive suite, how do you rate your networking style?**

   Circle your choice.

1	2	3	4	5	6	7	8	9	10
Not effective								**Extremely effective**	

   Explain _____

5. **Identify areas in which you need to improve your networking style.**

   _____   _____

   _____   _____

6. **In order to make your networking style more effective what do you think higher-ups would tell you to do or not do?**

   _____

Career Shaping Questions

7. **When it comes to sharing inside information that will give you the competitive edge, where do you draw the line in terms of sharing it with people who are competing for the same promotion as you?**

   _____

8. **How have you seen networking used in an inclusive way?**

   _____

9. **How have you seen networking used in an exclusive way?**

   _____

10. **Complete the following sentence.**

    Executives are best known for:

    1. _____   2. _____

    3. _____   4. _____

    Compare your answers with your boss's answers.

    What similarities exist_____

    What differences exist_____

11. **How much do you trust a person who says that politics never played a role in his or her promotion(s) to the top.**

1	2	3	4	5	6	7	8	9	10
    No Trust   **Fully Trust**

    Explain _____

Mentoring

Common Goal Mentoring vs. Extraordinary Mentoring

*Mentors...guide their disciples...imparting the wisdom they
have acquired over many years...Godfathers (sometimes called
"rabbis") are in a position to intervene on your behalf; by
definition, they are powerful people with an interest in your
career.*
                                                Mary Ann Allison

Originally, mentoring referred to a close relationship between a
senior staff person and a junior grade person. Exchanging information
or, as some would describe it, "tricks of the trade," were common
points of discussion. This led to the understudy being groomed
for a promotion and later repaying IOUs back to his or her mentor.
Today mentoring can mean almost anything that management and
staff desires it to be. In the main, it is used to guide a person's
progress. However, only a special type of mentoring leads to quick
and sure promotions. Unless the parties involved are sensitive to
the type of mentoring that is being given, misunderstandings can
ensue. This is why it is important to differentiate between common
goal mentoring intended for everyone and prestigious, extraordinary
mentoring designed exclusively for the heir-apparent.

All Mentoring Programs Are Not Created Equal

**In Common Goal Mentoring,
the trainee is called a mentee.**

vs.

**In Extraordinary Mentoring,
the trainee is called a protege.**

The difference between the two types of mentoring is both
quantitative and qualitative. At its highest point Common Goal
Mentoring enables people to become proficient in their assignments
- meeting minimum daily requirements. Maybe at its lowest point
Common Goal Mentoring shows people how to do just enough work
not to get fired or promoted.

Mentoring

Common Goal Mentoring
vs.
Extraordinary Mentoring

*When they (workers) choose a company, they often choose a
way of life. The (corporate) culture shapes their responses in
a strong, but substantial way. Culture can make them fast or
slow workers, tough or friendly managers, team players or
individuals. By the time they've worked for several years,
they may be so well conditioned by the culture they might not
even recognize it. But when they change jobs they may be in for
a big surprise.* Terrence E. Deal and Allan A. Kennedy

Extraordinary mentoring allows people to excel in their daily
work tasks and position themselves for advancement by joint
venturing with higher officials. Perhaps the key to the Extraordinary
Mentoring arrangement is the fact that both parties feel that they are
working towards a larger goal. A goal that unites them, but at the
same time transcends their relationship.

The Buddy System
a.k.a.
The Good Old Boys

**Frequently the end game between the mentor
and protege is the dual goal of improving the
organization while advancing one another up the
organization.**

Obviously, the results of linking up with a common goal mentor do
not compare to those achieved by teaming up with an extraordinary
career mentor. A super mentor can teach you the intricacies and the
unspoken rules of career advancement. In terms of moving up the
career ladder, which one do you want to spend more time with--a
Common Goal Mentor or an Extraordinary Mentor?

Common Goal Mentoring

Common Goal Mentoring vs. Extraordinary Mentoring

*One of the penalties for refusing to participate in politics
is that you end up being governed by your inferiors. Plato*

Common Goal Mentoring is a form of guidance and overseeing that ensures that the trainee understands his or her role in the organization. It involves an experienced employee leading a new worker through a phased-in orientation process. This provides the trainee with the practical experiences and strategies for getting the job done. The mentor oversees the worker's technical skills and pronounces him or her fit for duty.

The Model-T of Career Advancement

**The mission of the Common Goal Mentor is to make
sure you are competent at preforming your job.**

For the most part, Common Goal Mentoring is a ready-made type of mentoring that fulfills two needs. One is to provide employees with basic information on what the organization expects from them in terms of productivity and adherence to regulations. The second ensures that everyone has the skills needed to do his or her job. Since nearly every new employee receives this generic mentoring, it is another form of rudimentary supervision.

Super Mentoring
vs.
Basic Mentoring

**Unless the mentoring program goes beyond the
material presented in the procedural manuals it
remains an exercise in practical application.**

Common Goal Mentoring

Common Goal Mentoring
vs.
Extraordinary Mentoring

The common remark of top managers, "It's up to you here"
or "you can't keep a good man down" is often a cloak for
the fact that promotion is completely chancy and that merit
plays a subordinate role simply because no system for assessing
performance by men in junior and middle management exists.
Roy Lewis and Rosemary Stewart

In many cases, organizations have established training programs that concentrate more on Common Goal Mentoring and less on moving people into top management. Somehow it resembles a bait-and-switch con game. This can be a life changing moment. Do you jump out of the water like a fish taking the bait or do you become savvy in the ways of executive behavior?

Atta Boy

Common Goal Mentoring is presented as self empowerment, but it actually provides only limited autonomy in terms of decision making and how a person does his or her job.

While these mentoring efforts are appreciated, many employees feel misled by the fact that the so-called mentoring programs are heavy on technical training and light on executive-level promotions. In the reasoning of mentor programs, Common Goal Mentoring prepares a person to be a solid employee and not necessarily a leader, whose name is placed on the succession planning list for top management.

Extraordinary Mentoring

Common Goal Mentoring vs. Extraordinary Mentoring

Every member of the staff knew that if he aspired to higher office,
he must make a record of himself, a good part of which would be
a reputation among upper line officers of ability to "understand"
their informal problems without being told. Melville Dalton

10,000 hours of intense extraordinary mentoring at each rung on the career ladder will probably get you to the executive suite. It takes a super mentor to pronounce you fit for executive work and declare you worthy of competing against him or her for promotions. Managers handpick proteges and allow them to see power and control up close and personal. Mentoring provides tactical training and the key contacts that assure advancement. Actually, the gift of extraordinary mentoring is the gift that keeps on giving. Learning at the knee of the grand master enables a person to continually use someone else's wisdom, experience, and contacts to his or her own advantage.

Carrying The Torch For The Master

The mission of the extraordinary mentor is to make sure you get promoted to the executive suite. Mentors are ambitious for their friends to get promoted. They know that getting them promoted gives them friends in high places--friends they can call on for favors.

Scratch the surface of extraordinary mentoring and you will find hero worship. The personalized relationship between mentor and protege is built on mutual admiration, co-dependencies and commonalties. In effect, the two are loyal to one another's self interests and enable each other to advance in a leap frog fashion. This enabling process is predicated on the fact that both bring something special to the relationship that the other desires. The protege may have skills and contacts that are ideally suited for the mentor's needs. In return, the mentor provides custom designed assistance, superlative endorsements, and first-class links to top management. The bottom line is that promotions are based on hard work and scoring more political points than the other guy.

Extraordinary Mentoring

Common Goal Mentoring vs. Extraordinary Mentoring

In politics loyalty is everything. James Eastland

For these personal and professional reasons, the heir-apparent receives "preferential treatment" in work assignments that prepare him or her for advancement. Co-workers respond differently to the protege of a higher-up than they do to someone receiving Common Goal Mentoring. The individual is held in awe, and there is a tendency to defer to him for advice. In short, the protege is an extension of the mentor. He or she not only has more access to higher officials, but as a leader in training has more autonomy in the way that he does his or her job and makes decisions.

How to Become an Incredible and Awesome Executive

The so-called "Extraordinary Person" very likely began his or her career as a "good malleable worker" who attracted the attention of higher ups and received out-of-the-ordinary coaching and backing that made him or her appear to be in a class by him or herself. Voila! an "Extraordinary Executive" is created who meets the organization's needs.

Managers have a higher tolerance for the protege's mistakes, which are seen as part of the learning experience. Actually, mentoring at this level is a form of social and political Affirmative Action. It may not have the force of law, but it has the power of personality and social affinities, which resonates well with mentors looking for someone who reminds them of themselves.

The Original Affirmative Action Baby

The protege becomes the mentor's personal pet project for promotion to the executive suite.

Extraordinary Mentoring

Common Goal Mentoring vs. Extraordinary Mentoring

The slave has but one master, the ambitious man has as many masters as there are persons whose aid may contribute to the advancement of his fortune.   *J. De. Bruyere*

Mentors and proteges know that the best time to make friends is when you don't need them. If you want to advance, seek out people who can help you in the future. This is why mentoring relationships are important. The mentor serves as a trainer, advocate, and protector. With this support system in place, it is not unusual for the protege to eclipse the mentor's accomplishments and achieve a higher position. When this happens, the mentor has helped place someone in a position who can in turn provide him or her with assistance in the future. This is especially true if somewhere down the line the mentor needs a favor or is looking for employment. From this perspective, mentoring is a long term joint venture between a protege and management.

Back Scratching Is a State of Mind

Joint venture involves creating a partnership for performance. It allows the partners to pool their resources, reduce the risk of failure, and achieve success in a particular undertaking.

Got political capital? An uncommon mentor will help you in ways that you can never imagine. In extraordinary mentoring, the joint agenda between the mentor and protege emphasizes a spirit of "we're in this together." And therefore, we must make the most of our best talents to ensure each other's success up the career ladder.

The Paradox Of Mentoring

No man does anything from a single motive. Samuel Taylor Coleridge

Make Common Goal Mentoring available to everyone, but reserve extraordinary mentoring for people identified as proteges of top management.

Comparing The Mentoring Concepts

Me lift thee and thee life me, and we'll both ascent together.
J. G. Whittier

Common Goal Mentoring (Received by everyone)	**Extraordinary Mentoring** (Received by a chosen few)
Routine work relations with managers	So-called top talent receives a lot of face time with upper line officers e.g., personalized contacts
Receives competent training. Some one-on-one guidance, mostly group orientation	Pick of the bunch receives regal treatment. Best in personal and professional coaching
Information sources are so-so, second-hand grapevine rumors	Heir-expectant is privy to first-hand information
Career decisions made by trial-and-error process	Career decisions made via fast track insider information
Low autonomy regarding work and decision making	High autonomy regarding work and decision making
Acquires entry level job skills	Handpicked for special assignments and duties
Basic career guidance and support	Incomparable career planning and support for top promotions
Superior and subordinate roles are clearly delineated. Regular employees are not given extraordinary mentoring	Becoming the boss's aide-de-camp entitles one to be treated a "cut above" regular employees

Career Shaping Questions

1. **Write steps to deal with the Career Advancement Paradox of Mentoring, which states:**

    Make Common Goal Mentoring available to everyone, but reserve extraordinary mentoring for people identified as the "handpicked," favorites of top management.

    Step 1 _____

    Step 2 _____

    Step 3 _____

2. **List the pros and cons of this Career Advancement Paradox?**

Pros	Cons
_____	_____
_____	_____
_____	_____

3. **The boss always says "follow the rules." Would you like to have the rules for executive career advancement posted in the workplace for everyone to read and follow?**

    If yes, list the rules you want posted:

    _____

    If no, explain why.

    _____

Career Shaping Questions

4. **How have higher-ups and your peers dealt with the Paradox of Mentoring?**

   Explain _____

5. **Define Common Goal Mentoring (see pages 74, 75, 79).**

   _____

6. **Define Extraordinary Mentoring (see pages 76-79).**

   _____

7. **A powerful mentor is the best advantage. In the real world of fastball promotion politics and highly competitive (and sometimes nasty) career advancement, what formal and informal help do you expect from a well connected mentor?**

Formal help you want	**Informal help you want**
(up front where everyone can see it)	(behind the scenes where no one can see it)
_____	_____
_____	_____
_____	_____

Career Shaping Questions

8. **Are you currently receiving Common Goal Mentoring or Extraordinary Mentoring?**

   Explain _____

9. **"Just call me if you need any help," said the mentor to the rookie protege. How difficult is it for you to form a close relationship with a high level mentor (e.g., controls budget, staff, and resources) who is at your beck and call and will further your career by sharing secrets and advocating for your promotion to top management?**

   Circle your choice.

1	2	3	4	5	6	7	8	9	10
No difficulty							**Extremely difficult**		

   Explain _____

10. **To what degree are the values espoused by executives (honesty, integrity, and objectivity) reflected in the organization's promotion practices?**

    Circle your choice.

1	2	3	4	5	6	7	8	9	10

    Yes, the above values are always reflected in the organization's promotion practices.   **No, the above values are never reflected in the organization's promotion practices.**

    Explain _____

Strategic Promotion

Plateau vs. Advancement

*The top people, of the biggest companies, are surprisingly, often
the nicest ones in their company, I'm not sure, though, if they
got there because they were good guys or that they're now good
guys because they can afford to be. Malcolm Forbes*

Only a puzzle master can figure out how to fit together the pieces
that make up career advancement. To make things happen you have
to do contingency planning. Having a plan **A**, plan **B**, and plan
C allows you to better cope with uncertainty and bosses who can
be very capricious. Careerists know they must plan for the known
realities and the unexpected things that catch people off guard.

Strategic Thinking

A series of tactical maneuvers that allows people
to:
- **Out-execute the competition**
- **Deal effectively with transitions and change**
- **Focus on their objectives**
- **Understand their shortcomings and capabilities**
- **Maximize political capital -IOUs, pulling strings**
- **Re-invent themselves to meet new challenges**

Catching yourself strategizing to beat out the competition can
tell you a lot about yourself and how you find meaning in your
work. These revelations may lead some people to conclude
that career advancement is not for them at this time. They may
follow a strategem of plateauing or temporarily putting off career
advancement for personal or professional reasons. The following
page provides an overview of the reasons some people may pursue
career advancement aggressively and others do not.

Seek A Promotion Or Remain In Place

Factors Influencing Decision To Advance

Define politics as helping others while advancing oneself

Feel they have something unique to offer the organization

Thrive on having a lot of work responsibilities

Satisfying one's needs to be in charge and in control

Appreciate risk taking - aggressive, like power

Desire executive lifestyle - the best of everything

Like executive titles, status, prestige, center of attention

Earn a bigger pay check than everyone else

Savor political turf wars - getting even with peer rivals

Ensure the organization's survival - make safe changes

Pay back favors to mentors and supporters

Profit making before social responsibility

Factors Influencing Decision Not To Advance

Defining politics as an abomination and prostitution

Feel any personal efforts will not make a difference

The fewer work responsibilities the better

Uncomfortable charging to the front and taking control

Prefers to minimize - stress, strain, tension, burnout

Materialistic culture is false - principled

Career change, pursue educational or vocational goal

Money can't buy happiness

Strife, rivalry, striving for power are counter-productive

Organization prefers incremental changes, not reform

Feel integrity and ethics are always compromised

Social responsibility before profits

The Concept Of Plateauing

Plateau vs. Advancement

*The race may not be to the swift nor the victory to
the strong, but that's how you bet. Damon Runyou*

In searching for a satisfactory balance between life and work,
some people may decide to settle into a position "for the long haul"
and not seek advancement. Not wanting to assume additional
responsibilities may be a sign that he or she knows his or her
limitations. Periods of non-advancement may also be due to real
barriers, i.e., health factors, family considerations, or completing
educational programs.

Is The Glass Ceiling Forever?

**In some cases a stalled career may be due to artificial
barriers that prevent some people from rising above
a pre-set level in the organization.**

Some people can see through the proverbial glass ceiling but can't
seem to get above it. Another aspect of the plateauing process may
include management's conclusion that someone is not a good fit
for the organization. This individual may be placed in a dead-end
position as a way to terminate his or her career or to nudge him or
her to move on. Claiming to have years of experience and depth
of vision, the decision makers decide how they can best use an
individual's professional and personal talents. They may feel that
a person has peaked out early in his or her career and track him or
her into positions that have limited opportunities. In other situations
they may sense that it's to their advantage to promote a particular
person. Some people decide to advance and others may elect to
forego climbing the ladder of success. Given the changing nature
of career advancement, an individual must, in his or her own way,
come to terms with the concepts of plateauing and advancing.

Causes of Career Plateauing
As Defined by Management

Life is a game played on us while we are playing other games.
Evan Esar

•

• • • •

• • • • • • • •

No team skills

No political savvy

Makes the boss look bad

Leaks confidential information

Never follows the chain of command

Personal decision not to climb career ladder

Disregards or mocks the organization's traditions

Not cooperating fully with boss's protege and supervisors

Boss does not feel person "fits in" with organization's culture

Unwilling to charm, humor, and show proper deference to superiors

The Concept of Advancement

Plateau vs. Advancement

Our life always expresses the result of our dominant thought.
S. Kierkegarrd

If you want to get ahead in this world you have to work hard. In other words, one moves up by simply doing his or her job. However, in the mind of the careerist, this sweet homily begs the question "Work hard at what?" Working hard at career politics or work tasks? The intensely ambitious know that both are necessary. Given that most people practice a hard work ethic, the focus is on career politics which is the mothers milk of career advancement.

Connect the Political Dots

Working hard at career politics refers to one's ability to put together the relationship dots that control the workplace.

The mettlesome challenge is to connect the personal dots with the professional dots. And then join those dots with the political dots that help one to link up with the needs of the higher-ups. Discussing the connection between the power dots of career advancement and politics tends to polarize people into two camps. There are those who believe in using politics and those who don't. Yet, despite all the talk denouncing politics, the essence of advancement lies in one's ability to make informed choices that will move one ahead of his or her competitors. This requires straight talk about Career Advancement between management and staff.

Master of the Zig Zag

Anything less than straight talk results in the dumbing down of Career Advancement Politics.

The Concept of Advancement

It pays to size up the boss, because he or she is sizing you up in more ways than you can imagine. L.Flores

A well connected person is someone who has made a mental link between the power brokers and his or her needs. He or she then artfully works these tie-ins for all they are worth. Advancement comes down to being able to decipher the unspoken and unwritten connections that only the ambitious can see, hear, or imagine. Can you connect your workplace power dots?

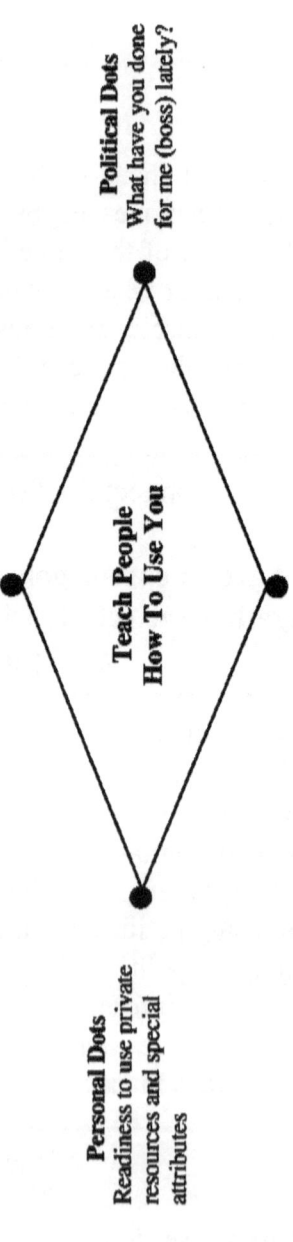

Management Needs Dots
How alert are you to identify the boss's professional or personal goals?

Political Dots
What have you done for me (boss) lately?

Teach People How To Use You

Professional Dots
How willing are you to use your acquired skills and expertise to help the boss achieve his or her goals?

Personal Dots
Readiness to use private resources and special attributes

The Concept of Advancement

Now that I'm almost up the ladder
I should, no doubt, be feeling gladder
It is quite fine, the view and such
If just it didn't shake so much.
Richard Armour

Nothing says career advancement like a well planned, well fought for and well earned promotion. Nearly everyone wants to achieve a position or title that reflects his or her highest ambitions. As people move up the career ladder, they know that more is expected of them, both personally and professionally. They must pass the unspoken test of utility, which makes a point of saying:

There Are No Free Lunches
Nothing Is Free

**What can you do for me (the organization)
that the other candidates can't?**

Example_____

On one level, the question above relates to professional competencies. On another level it fleshes out individual skills that indicate how useful your personal talents, abilities, and connections will be to the organization. It measures not only how well you will fit in, but how receptive you are to the needs of the organization's leaders. Answering this unspoken question correctly and discreetly not only distinguishes a person from the "also ran," but also prepares him or her to deal with the informal organization. One secret of advancement is knowing how to make workplace politics work for you instead of against you. This is done by knowing that success entails a special aptitude for coming up with strategies that increase one's circle of influence and positions one to be pre-selected for the next promotion. Central to all this is the question—can you rise to the boss's needs both professionally and personally?

The Concept Of Advancement

A man with a career can have no time to waste upon his wife
and friends, he has to devote it wholly to his enemies.
John Oliver Hobbes

Once promoted, a lot of people start preparing for their next promotion. To this end, they apply more tactical thinking and make the most out of what their current position has to offer. It becomes a stepping stone to the next promotion. The plan is to continually pre-position himself or herself and achieve promotions that result in: Freedom, Power, Opportunity, and Reciprocity.

1. Freedom
Men are never so likely to settle a question rightly
as when they discuss it freely. Lord Macaulay

Executives claim that they like the decision-making latitude that comes with a leadership position. Although accountability exists, the executive to a considerable degree has the independence to run things as he or she sees fit. This is popularly called "being your own person." The concept of "always being yourself" has a rugged individualist appeal, but in reality it is hard for an executive to always be in this mode when he or she is continually bombarded by multiple stress factors. Despite their autonomy, executives find that they are never free of the push and pull of politics.

2. Power
Power is the ultimate aphrodisiac. Henry A. Kissinger

The cornerstone of power is the ability to have a commanding influence on all things in the organization. Purely and simply, it is having the clout to make or impact decisions at whatever level is desired. Whether it's called a game or a business decision, it comes down to finding ways to accumulate enough control and authority to sway opinions on matters that are deemed important.

The Concept Of Advancement

*The price one pays for pursuing any profession
or calling is an intimate knowledge of its ugly side.*
James Baldwin

3. Opportunities
Manage the opportunities that change offers.
Performance Science Corp.

Seeking new ideas, probing for information, and creating something innovative are the hallmarks of success. By uniquely combining facts, needs, desires, and circumstances, a person can position himself or herself to be seen as a leader. This gets the attention of higher-ups and exemplifies well judged risk taking, which can promote a person's career. Higher officials value people who have a creative spirit and who are open to accepting career guidance. In the end it is opportunities we have received and opportunities we have missed that determines how far we move up the career ladder.

4. Reciprocity
A man's most open actions have a secret side to them. Joseph Conrad

You owe me one! This statement seems to encapsulate a state of mind that prevails among many staff members. Using people and being used is something everyone does in one form or another. However, most people prefer to redefine it as helping people out, or just saying "may I help you." Not paying back favors can generate pangs of guilt and shame. It seems that collecting IOUs and repaying IOUs is the currency of exchange in organizations. This opens the door to gift giving and doing favors for others. It brings in the expectation that favors will be repaid in like kind or on a greater scale. Besides building trust and loyalty between staff members, it is a way of bartering and honing one's gamesmanship skills. Reciprocity must be understood as the bedrock of humanity and survival. It turns on the willingness of one person to help another person, who in turn gives back. This is the essence of teaching people how to use their skills, talents, and resources.

The Concept Of Advancement
Plateau vs. Advancement

Put your emotional life in order...
It's a great help in climbing towards the higher
rungs of the career ladder, to be happy in life,
rather than find yourself mired in emotional crisis.
It's hard enough to succeed without taking on
personal problems that sap your energy and divert
your attention.   *Michael Korda*

In summary, the charge to the top of the organization requires a person to have a "gung ho" careerist attitude which borders on irrational exuberance. This drives a person to:

- Pass through the eye of a rusty needle-ability to tolerate all out scrutiny
- Be a teflon chameleon-Don't take anything personally and know how to blend in
- Be a competitive problem solver-out smart, out perform and out shine rivals
- Spin straw into gold-ability to turn adversity into a golden opportunity
- Be a plate spinner-Stamina to keep 20 plates spinning on 20 sticks at one time without breaking a sweat or a plate

Strategic Promotion Dual Paradoxes

By working faithfully eight hours a day you may eventually
get to be boss and work twelve hours a day.
Robert Frost

1. Be 100% dedicated to your family's needs and 100% dedicated to the organization's needs.

2. Attract people to you. Create the persona of being compassionate and fair-minded, but when you spot a weakness, don't hesitate to go for the jugular.

Overview Of Plateau
and
Strategic Promotion Process

*By the time you rise through the ranks, the culture of
homogenization has bred the spirit of imagination out of you.*
Ralph Nader

Every career step requires a person to make decisions that dictate the speed and direction of his or her advancement. The list below provides a view of the plateau factors that slow progress and the advancement factors that can accelerate a person's career.

Plateau	Advancement
Slow Track	Fast Track
Career is #3 or 4 in priorities. Resolutely holds to personal values - uncompromising.	Career is #1 life priority. Epitomizes the ideal organization man or woman - flexible style.
Inclined to be more loyal to family than to organization.	Inclined to be more loyal to the organization than to family.
Individual decides to temporarily place his or her career on hold.	Finds a way to use every opportunity for upward mobility.
Artificial barriers (glass ceiling) hinder career progress. Real barriers (health, education) impact career progress.	Utilizes personal and professional contacts to overcome barriers. Absolute commitment to the organization's agenda.
Organization decides not to advance a person. Promotion passover is used to address personal needs.	Finds formal and informal ways to exceed expectations. Merges work style with the organization's needs. Looks for ways to increase skills and resources.

Career Shaping Questions

1. **Write steps to deal with the Career Advancement Dual Paradoxes of Strategic Promotion, which states:**

    A. **Be 100% dedicated to your family's needs and 100% dedicated to the organization's needs.**

    B. **Attract people to you. Create the persona of being compassionate and fair-minded, but when you spot a weakness don't hesitate to go for the jugular.**

    Step 1 _____

    Step 2 _____

    Step 3 _____

2. **Evaluate the pros and cons of this Career Advancement Paradox.**

Pros	Cons
_____	_____
_____	_____
_____	_____

Career Shaping Questions

3. **How have higher-ups and your peers dealt with the Dual Paradoxes of Strategic Promotion?**

   Explain _____

4. **How do your family values (things honored, esteemed, respected, appreciated) match the organization's values?**

   List your family values

   _____   _____

   _____   _____

   List your organization's values

   _____   _____

   _____   _____

   Value System
   List values that your family and organization
   have in common

   _____   _____

   _____   _____

Career Shaping Questions

5. Upward mobility is directly proportionate to how much quality time a person invests in his or her career. Circle the approximate percentage of time you spend on your career per month. Include working hours and outside work-related activities, e.g., overtime, taking work home, socializing with co-workers - talking shop.

   0%   5   10   20   30   40   50   60   70   80   90   100%

6. In terms of your career advancement, where do you see yourself five years from now?

   _____

7. In terms of your family situation, where do you see yourself five years from now?

   _____

8. Complete the following sentence

   Ambitious career climbers are best known for:

   1. _____   2. _____

   3. _____   4. _____

   Compare your answers with your boss's answers.

   What similarities exist_____

   What differences exist_____

Overview Of Career Advancement Theory

Defining Moments	Dynamics	Promotion Paradoxes
Background	Fully Qualified *vs.* Preferred Qualifications	Simultaneously have the right subjective and objective qualifications
Acceptance	Conditional vs. Unconditional	Always be yourself, but emulate the characteristics of top management.
Opportunity	Low Profile vs. High Profile	All at the same time, welcome low profile opportunities but pursue high profile opportunities. Learn how to disguise high profile opportunities as low profile.
Networking	Exclusion vs. Inclusion	Information is for sharing, but reserve best information for personal advantage
Mentoring	Common Goal Mentoring vs. Extraordinary Mentoring	Make mentoring accessible to everyone, but reserve fast track for management's proteges.
Strategic Promotion	Plateau vs Advancement	Be 100% dedicated to your family and 100% dedicated to the organization. Have a caring persona, but when you see a weakness go for the jugular.

Summary: The Real World Model

If A is success in life, than A equals X plus Y plus Z. Work is X, Y is play and Z is keeping your mouth shut.

Albert Einstein

Career Advancement Equation

$$HW + A + C + {}^*X\ Factor = CA$$

Hard Work	+	Appearances	+	Connections	+	X Factor	=	Career Advancement
Key elements		Key elements		Key elements		Key elements		Key elements
						Qualities subjectively defined by higher-ups		
Self-starter		Impeccable image		Ties to VIPs		Performance		Model executive
Iron will		Drive car with snob appeal		Lodge brother		Potential		Success driven
Game to the end		High-end neighborhood		Fraternity/sorority		Likeability		Profit oriented
Indefatigable		Large vocabulary		Private clubs		Savoir-faire		Relentless achiever
Stick-to-itive		Charismatic		Partnerships		Personality fits-in		Perfect fit for the job
Never idle		Character, values, ethics		Bond with boss		Professionally fits-in		Brilliant business acumen

*X Factor see pages 5, 11, 16, 36, 112, 126, 135

Career Shaping Questions

Career Advancement Equation

$$HW + A + C + X\ Factor = CA$$

How does the Career Advancement Equation play itself out in your workplace? Under each of the words below fill-in the key elements which you feel determine how people are promoted. See page 98 for examples.

Hard Work List Elements	+	**Appearances** List Elements	+	**Connections** List Elements	+	*** X Factor** List elements as subjectively defined by boss and higher-ups	=	**Career Advancement** List elements
____		____		____		____		____
____		____		____		____		____
____		____		____		____		____

As a group exercise compare your list with your co-workers' list. Prioritize the key elements and develop an action plan that will create and maintain a level playing field for everyone.

* X Factor see pages 5, 9, 10, 11, 16

Summary: The Real World Model

Man by nature is a political animal. Aristotle (384-322 B.C.)

The bottom line to the politics of promotion is that career advancement is predicated on the terms, conditions, and paradoxes created by upper management. Often times, self-preservation in a competitive organization requires you to think intuitively and counter intuitively. Intuitive thinking allows you to reason things out logically and orderly. Counter intuitive thinking allows you to brain storm from the sublime to the surreal and challenge assumptions so you can anticipate situations before they occur. Mastering the promotion paradoxes requires us to see things as they are and not as we want them to be. This points to the need for a body of knowledge specific to the politics of promotion. People need tools that will allow them to x-ray what is going on in the name of career development. The thrust of the model is to examine the intrinsic realities of promotion politics and set forth an alternative to the Conventional Wisdom Models. While we must respect traditional values, we must also press forward in order to realize the full potential for fairness that exists in the workplace. Whether one is promoted or assigned a new boss, the process of proving oneself at all levels of the Real World Model starts over.

Are You Executive Caliber?

**Proving one's self as defined by others
in the workplace is a never-ending process.**

It takes competence and courage to do what needs to be done to achieve an edge over the competition. With every new promotional situation the rules vary until the right combination of personal and professional skills is found to handle the changes that confront a person. Certainly, a 360-degree perspective on career advancement politics can help clarify things. This view can be achieved when individuals apply the following: 1. Leaders must treat career advancement politics as a topic of vital importance. 2. Organizations must embrace cultural diversity as an asset to the staff and their profit centers.

Summary: Real World Model

We eat reality sandwiches. Allen Ginsberg

1. Leaders must treat career advancement politics as a topic of vital importance

Ironically, leaders, to one degree or another, must politic in order to move up the career ladder, but many shy away from an in-depth discussion of the political skills needed to move ahead. Failing to seriously discuss the politics of promotion results in resentment toward management and harms the work team's esprit de corps. To avoid this, three things must occur: (1) Career Advancement Politics must be accepted as a discipline, (2) management must discuss it with staff, and (3) the politics of promotion must be integrated into organizational behavioral concepts. Unless this occurs, many dedicated staff members tend to lose faith in the organization's promotion system. This moves many staff to make the following statement of concern:

Don't just tell me what you did, tell me how you did it.

---

2. Organizations must embrace cultural diversity as an asset to the staff and their profit centers

Many organizations give cultural diversity a sophisticated form of lip service. Some have turned it into a great public relations tool. Managers may see it as a set of slick techniques for sales and marketing to people of color. Others make a big deal of bringing in motivational speakers to give inspirational speeches, but nothing really significant changes. For example, the promotion of women and people of color to CEO is a rarity. To achieve success in a multi-cultural workplace, diversity must be actively practiced. Ideally, it must lead to parity in recruitment, hiring, training, retention and promotion of women, people of color and people from other disenfranchised groups into key executive positions.

Chapter 3

The Conventional Wisdom Models
for
Career Advancement

*The conventional view serves to protect us
from the painful job of thinking. John Kenneth Galbraith*

Rugged Individualism
Pull Yourself Up by Your Bootstraps

When discussing career advancement the above cliche
is one of management's favorites. It implies that
executives make it to the top on their own merits and
virtues and that politics are for the weak minded.

"I made it to the top on my own." Political Translation:
"I worked hard and politicked hard to find people who
could pull me up to the top."

The Conventional Wisdom Models
For Career Advancement

Life is a zoo in a jungle. Peter de Viries

How do I become an executive? This question goes to the heart, soul, and DNA of career politics and career advancement. Lacking a clear-cut way to discuss all the facets of promotion politics, management utilizes two approaches to answer this persistent question. One is to openly discuss career advancement via the three Conventional Wisdom Models presented in this chapter:

The Traditional Career Path Model: The Perfect Myth
The Content Of Character Model
The Sports Model

Generally, these well crafted models employ a carrot-and-stick approach to explain the basis for promotions. They offer the hope of a promotion to staff and are used to keep personnel problems to a minimum. Management has found them to be an excellent way to talk about advancement without using the ubiquitous word *politics*. They have become standard, boilerplate thinking when it comes to explaining promotions. The hoped for result of this indoctrination is that staff will embrace them as their personal career models. However, the question pops up: To what degree do they represent the sum and substance of what it takes to advance? So much energy has gone into creating and maintaining the Conventional Wisdom Models that it is difficult to contest them. Devoted followers swear that if certain steps are followed a person will be promoted. They seem enamored with the idea that the models are part popular thinking and part folk tales with a calming effect on the way that people perceive and ask questions about career advancement.

Conventional Wisdom Models
Ideas, hunches, and hopes passed from one generation to another generation.

Folklore Message
Unquestioned myth, lore, and notions. Home spun yarns-tall tales.

It requires a very unusual mind to make an analysis of the obvious.
Alfred N. Whitehead

The second approach to explaining career advancement politics employs contemporary as well as trendy new career development training. Management may use them as a foil to avoid dealing with career politics. Thus, well meaning consultants may be witting or unwitting accomplices to management's political agenda. Staff feel that they get the royal run around because career development and career politics are two different topics. However, it suits management's needs to merge them together. Sure enough, this approach raises more questions than answers because it lacks a bona fide political thrust that gets to the meat of promotion politics.

Are They Selling The Sizzle Or The Steak?

Pop-culture management fads, quick-fix-ideas, warm fuzzy inspirational books, and peacock motivational speakers are sold as the solution to career advancement problems. Predictably, they present safe, traditional topics and tell people that hard work is the only way to the executive suite. They fail to directly address the politics of promotion. Thus, career advancement politics remains a troublesome, hard core issue.

With the passage of time the popular wisdom concepts seem to have become a fixed ideology that many people, for lack of an alternative point of view, have come to believe. As if it was the path to illumination or a gift from the gods of management, executives use the Conventional Wisdom Models and the latest-in-vogue training techniques to get the staff to buy into the organization's career advancement philosophy. In other words, buy the sizzling hyperbole and not the true facts of career politics. This is misguided and it often backfires on management. Therefore, this chapter x-rays the Conventional Wisdom that is used to explain how people are promoted.

The Perfect Myth:
The Traditional Career Path Model

*I have abandoned my search for the truth and am now looking
for a good fantasy.*   *Ashleigh Brilliant*

Do you want to be promoted? Just work hard, keep your nose
to the grindstone, and you will be discovered and promoted. This
is the premise of the Traditional Career Path Model, which has five
interlocking steps. Each step represents an undisputable truism,
deeply anchored in the American work ethic. For example, no one
will dispute the first step, which holds that education is the key to
advancement. Secondly, it seems disrespectful to go against the
time honored ideas and legacies handed down by the organization's
founding fathers. As a model for career advancement, the Traditional
Career Path Model has survived unscathed for centuries. This book
examines the strengths and weak points of this model. For openers,
the model seems to represent management's ideologically preferred
approach for setting up promotions by "getting all your ducks in a
row." This metaphor implies that things go much easier when they
are carefully lined up, so that all goes your way and appears just as
you want it to be. And no one is the wiser. Given that executives take
to politics like ducks take to water, the aforementioned expression
about ducks is apropos.

Playing On People's Fears

**The fact that people are reluctant to question the
premise of the Traditional Career Path Model assures
it a permanent place in the organization's culture.**

Some organizations bank on the idea that people will never
openly question their executives about the politics of promotions.
Rather than be considered troublemakers, many people opt to say
nothing. Therefore, the Traditional Career Path Model for Career
Advancement remains a simplistically attractive concept that is easy
to recite and readily comprehensible.

The Traditional Career Path Model: The Perfect Myth

Since the masses are always eager to believe something for their benefit, nothing is so easy as to arrange the facts.
Charles Maurice de Talleyrand

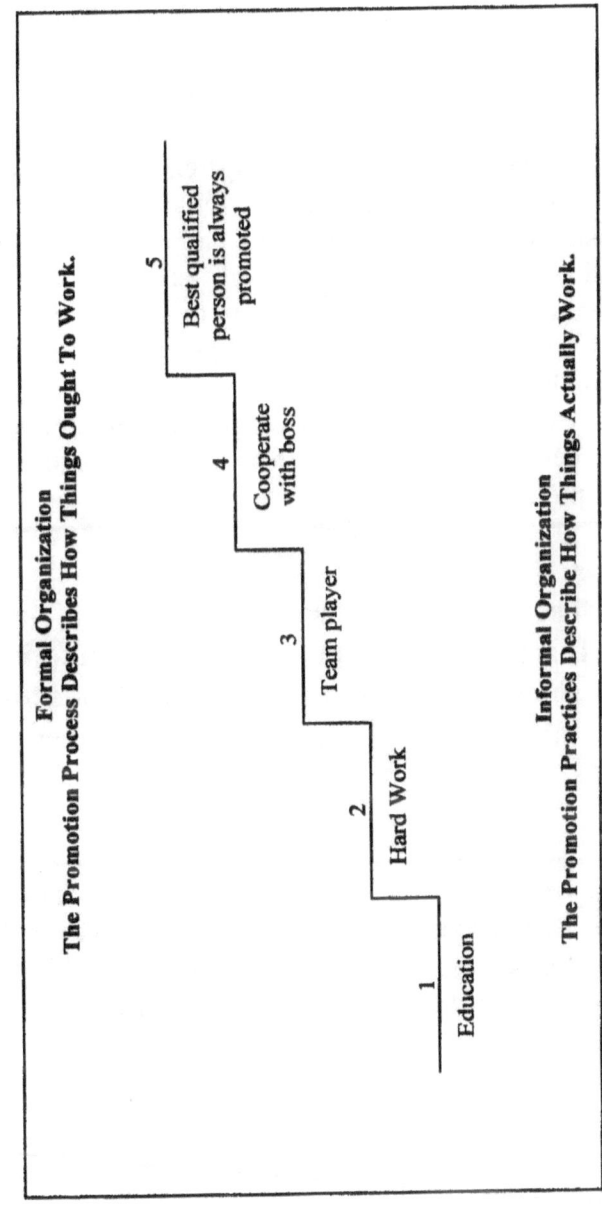

Formal Organization
The Promotion Process Describes How Things Ought To Work.

1 — Education
2 — Hard Work
3 — Team player
4 — Cooperate with boss
5 — Best qualified person is always promoted

Informal Organization
The Promotion Practices Describe How Things Actually Work.

The Perfect Myth:
The Traditional Career Path Model

Seek simplicity and then distrust it. Alfred Whitehead

A strong work ethic and competence are the keys to advancement. This is what has been traditionally told to employees by persons in positions of authority, such as parents, teachers, military leaders, and politicians. It seems more expedient to put forth homilies than to do introspective thinking that might conflict with one's pat answers. Unfortunately, "pat answers" to complex problems breed complacency or acrimony. Convenient homilies that patronize staff and exaggerate the virtues and rewards of hard work and obfuscate the benefits of politics must be avoided because they set the stage for problems.

---

*KISS IT
The Traditional Career Path Model is simplicity itself.
It is grounded in the belief that promotions are based
solely on how well a person performs his or her job.
***K**eep **I**t **S**imple, **S**weetheart
or
Keep **I**t **S**imple, **S**tupid

The belief system presented by the Traditional Career Path Model has been handed down from one generation to another and draws its staying power from two facts: One is that this pet model is made up of truisms that are hard to refute. The second is that it is deeply ingrained in popular thought as "the one true way" by which all leaders and executives abide.

Trust Me, I'm Your Spiritual Leader

The Traditional Career Path Model wins followers
because it is presented as the natural and
organizationally prescribed way of getting ahead.

Step 1. Education

Formal education will make you a living:
self-education will make you a fortune. Jim Rohn

Making the grade is what education and career advancement are all about. The educational system with its hierarchy of grades instills in people certain rules for getting ahead. The classical conditioning process for climbing bureaucratic hierarchies and achieving socioeconomic rewards starts early in life. Children grasp the idea that in order to advance to a higher level they must do as told by their superiors. Some go from teacher's pet to political animal.

> **Education is a positive force; however, it has a way of teaching students that their future lies in their ability to please those who evaluate their progress.**

Students who conform to the rules are promoted up the educational pyramid. Thus, many students arrive at the workplace pre-programed with the idea that they will be promoted when the boss sees what a great job they are doing. Other students learn to appreciate the system's formal and informal ways of doing things (bring an apple for the teacher) and transfer this thinking to the workplace, where they compete and easily out-think their peer rivals. In our credential-oriented society, education is a major necessity. Rightly or wrongly, we're all in a paper chase. We are afflicted with diploma disease, which means that having the right piece of paper helps one to achieve his or her goals. To those eager to get ahead this means "get promoted or perish."

> **For the masses of people obtaining degrees, certificates, and licenses, the academic learning process is presented as the great equalizer.**

Education is a formal equalizer. But it does not ensure survival in the informal Machiavellian culture of status, power, and control.

Step 1. Education

*If you feel that you have both feet planted on level
ground, then the university has failed you. R. Goheen*

Formal learning ensures that people entering the workforce have the
right work skills, people pleasing techniques, and knowledge base.
Secondarily, education shows that the person has been conditioned
to work with others, meet deadlines, and take constructive criticism.
To many people, this translates into the idea that the doors of success
will literally slam wide-open once they have a degree in their hand.

Old School Thinking
College Degree + Job + Hard Work = Promotion

New School Thinking
College Degree + Job + Hard Work + X Factor = Promotion

There exist a unique social contract between students and academic
programs (Leadership, Public Administration, Human Resources,
Business, Management, Organizational Behavior) that offer
executive development skills. For recruitment and retention, it
is in the interest of colleges to create programs that help students
become politically competent in managing and confronting the
politics of promotion.

We must value the formal education process, but recognize its
limitations and institutional blind spots when it comes to career
politics. Colleges provide an education for earning a living; they do
not deliver an education in career advancement. Ironically, this is
what many people need in order to survive in today's workplace. A
first-class education enlightens and stimulates growth by listening
and asking questions. A second-class education keeps people half
informed and hobbled by old cliches and conventional beliefs about
career advancement. Unless there are courses in career politics,
students have no tangible framework to use as a guide. They are at
the mercy of the boss's promotion practices and possibly at risk of
becoming cynical and distrusting toward higher ups.

Step 2. Hard Work

Competence, like truth, beauty and contact lenses,
is in the eye of the beholder.
Laurence Peters

In the United States, the first Monday in September is Labor Day. This is an annual renewal of the country's commitment to continual progress and a way of proclaiming its superior work ethic. Colorful parades depict a culture that revels in high performance, work, and playing hard. Speeches extol the idea that it was hard work that made this country great. Shrines and memorials are dedicated to the ideals of workmanship and craftsmanship. From this spring loyalty and a patriotic duty to emulate, if not compete with, and outdo our ancestor's successes. This is ingrained in the following popular sayings, which magnify and express the philosophy of self-sacrifice and toil.

True or False	T	F
Hard work is its own reward.	——	——
You can't keep a good man down.	——	——
I let my work do the talking for me.	——	——
Where there is a will there is a way.	——	——
I worked hard to get to my position.	——	——
Work hard and good things will happen.	——	——
I did it the old-fashioned way; I earned it.	——	——
I give a full day's work for a full day's pay.	——	——
Nothing comes to those who don't work hard.	——	——

Industriousness, productivity, and fierce independence are words often used to describe the American national character. These attributes symbolize the country's past achievements and highlight its present accomplishments. As befitting a workforce, which sees itself as cutting-edge progressive, we take great pride in our hard driving ability to make advances.

Step 2. Hard Work

Work is love made visible. Kahlil Gibran

Many people have a heart-felt passion for work because it provides a sense of fulfillment and meaning in life. Hard work is valued because it is comprised of actions that give substance to a person's efforts to achieve his or her goals. In its purest form, as many feel it was meant to be, hard work is devoid of promotion politics. Many prefer to feel that success is based on merit and developing one's God-given talents and abilities.

> **There is a long held trust that if a person does a "first-rate" job he or she will be advanced on the merits of his or her efforts.**

The term "hard worker" generally refers to qualities such as competence, performance, and skills. It can also describe a tough minded, matter-of-fact person who handles difficult tasks effectively and efficiently.

> **To the true believer, "kissing up" is a repugnant act and is incompatible with the spirit of a hard work ethic.**

From this flows the notion that if a person works hard, he or she will be discovered and promoted without using clever, self-serving tactics. From a hard work perspective, performance is the sole standard of measurement for deciding who is advanced up the career ladder. People who place their faith in hard work and ultimately see little or no promotions forthcoming become disillusioned. They feel that politically based promotions cancel out or at least diminish the benefits of having a hard work ethic.

Step 3. Teamwork

Teamwork is consciously espoused but unwittingly shunned
by most people in business because they are deathly afraid of it.
They think it will render them anonymous, invisible.

Srully Blotnick

In its most ideal form teamwork is about working with people you love to be around. This wishful thinking is expressed in the phrase "we're one big happy family" at work. A sense of camaraderie and giving one's best for the good of the group are the things that bind people together. For many people, trying to fit into the various work groups becomes a job in and of itself. No one wants to be left out, so working with others becomes a "learn as you go" process in order to earn the group's respect.

Make People Feel Important

"Hitting it off well" with the work team and making contributions results in positive peer group approval.

Example _____

Fulfilling these "must do's" (socializing, proving yourself, securing the confidence of the group) is critical for people aspiring to move up. In return, they believe that the work group treats everyone as "one of the family" and is supportive of their efforts to advance. The uncanny thing about teamwork is that with the passage of time, only one individual's name becomes synonymous with the group's accomplishments. As the years go by, the highest positioned team leader seems to emerge as the person responsible for the project and gets the credit and top billing. The rest of the hard toiling team players receive honorable mention. Eventually, the team is disbanded and becomes a footnote in the organization's history. Never confuse getting high marks as a team player with career advancement. Team work is about cooperating with co-workers. Career advancement is about being selected the best team player by the boss and co-workers. An ambitious team player is able to subtly get others to endorse him or her as the most valuable player.

Step 4. Cooperate With The Boss

Point of view is worth 80 IQ points. Alan Kay

Are you ready, willing, and able to tweak the boss's ego? In the United States, October sixteenth is celebrated as National Boss Day. April twenty-fifth is acclaimed as Administrative Professional Day. Besides the commercial value that these days bring, they symbolize the link between workers and those who lead them. The existence of National Boss Day attests to the fact that workers recognize the boss's role and contributions. Or, at least find inventive ways to keep the boss in good spirits so that relationships can remain as friction free as possible.

Fill In the Blanks
and
Read between the lines of the Position Description.
Part of your job is to make the boss look good.

Example _____

Whatever else you do, make the boss appear like an intelligent and wise leader. Up and down the career ladder, this is known as "staying on the boss's good side." For example, it's been said with satire and irony that when a person's opinions agree with those of the boss, he or she is considered to be well informed. Depending on the condition and size of their egos, bosses may press home the need to feel superior; otherwise they would not be addressed and referred to as "your superiors." Without saying it, a lot of bosses sometimes think they are the smartest persons in the room. Recognizing that the boss has the final word and making him or her look smart is just the start of pre-positioning oneself for advancement. The nature of power relationships requires that one support the boss and defer to a higher-up's authority, experience, and title. In turn, bosses, in theory, exercise their power, influence, and control over workers in an evenhanded way. The care and feeding of the boss is important. Many people do creative things to make him or her feel like a legion in their own time.

Step 4. Cooperate With The Boss

People ask the difference between a leader and a boss...
The leader leads, and the boss drives. Theodore Roosevelt

Usually, there is a direct correlation between how much bosses feel they can trust an individual and how much supervision that person receives. Supposedly, the more reliable a person is, the more freedom he is given in carrying out his or her work.

Do You Comply Out of Fear or Respect?

Nothing impresses the boss more than knowing that when all is said and done you yield to his or her request.

I conform out of: Respect ___ Fear ___ Other ___

Explain _____

This tells the people in charge that you understand the concept of top-to-bottom control and the spirit of following orders. In the end, the boss has the final word. Subordinates who abide by this rule show that they know their place in the chain of command and in the relationship between superiors and underlings.

I Am House Broken

Showing that one is appropriately submissive and compliant can be an asset in career advancement.
Circle your choice
False   1   2   3   4   5   6   7   8   9   10   True

Explain_____

Step 5.
The Best-Qualified Person Is Always Promoted

The view only changes for the lead dog.
Sergeant Preston of the Yukon

Most organization executives like to "strut their stuff" by saying "we run a tight ship here." They announce how proud they are of their organization's exemplary promotion process. They tend to say things like "Our promotion process is second to none when it comes to fairness." Or, executives will enthusiastically proclaim that "Your career is in good hands with our managers; they have the courage to always do the right thing." Words to this effect are intended to inspire total confidence in the organization's upper leadership. And they play extremely well with a lot of people. For example, those recently promoted are held up as living proof that the organization always promotes the right person. This is because management wants to always appear competent and their credibility is riding on selecting the right person at the right time for the right job. No matter what, the boss's actions must always equate to fairness and leadership.

Political Flashpoints

Testimonials from newly minted executives seem to support the idea that performance is all that matters and that politics never played a role in their advancement.

No matter how illusory this model may appear, it has found a place in the hearts and minds of many people. It has crystallized the idea that only "the creme de la creme" succeed. It is of paramount importance that supporters of the Traditional Career Path Model accept this conclusion and propagate it among themselves. Without this unified front, the seeds of lasting discontent and well founded doubt regarding the organization's promotions practices will begin to sprout.

Weak Point #1
The Traditional Career Path Model
Fails to Address the
Needs of Today's Workforce

People who have the power to make things happen don't do the things that people do, so they don't know what needs to happen.
Russell Baker

The Traditional Career Path Model is well-intentioned, but it does not respond to the changing realities of the workplace. Work was once considered a relatively safe haven from social, class, political, ethnic, gender, and economic issues. It's now an active incubator for these issues and requires a different set of philosophical beliefs from management and staff. This is witnessed by the fact that:

Today's Employees

Are culturally diverse
Know their civil rights
Are geographically mobile
Have high career expectations
Are quick to question authority figures
Are better educated and possess street survival skills

If executives want their staff to maintain good morale and high productivity levels, they must not overlook or minimize the problems caused by career politics. It is important to see things through the eyes of a person who may feel disfranchised. Organizations are begging for turmoil when management ignores the problems caused by promotion politics. If organizations want more loyal staff members, executives must know where they stand on the issue of promotion politics and how their actions come across to their staff. Leaders who avoid doing political reality checks pay a high price for neglecting to examine the impact of promotion politics on the staff's esprit de corps.

Weak Point #1
The Traditional Career Path Model
Fails to Address the Needs of Today's Workforce

There are no whole truths; all truths are half truths, It is trying
to treat them as whole truths that plays the devil.
Alfred North Whitehead

To understand their staff's career expectations, organizations must assess how their executive managers think and rationalize their promotion decisions. To this end they can:

1. Deny that politics has anything to do with promotions
2. Affirm their belief in the Traditional Career Path Model
3. Openly work to discuss and eliminate promotion politics

Unfortunately, when answering the question "how do I get promoted," executives tend to tout the virtues of the Traditional Career Path Model. This is counterproductive to the openness that the staff expects and is seen as insincere when it comes to helping people develop their careers. Executives cannot afford to be locked into such deceptively innocent sounding concepts as The Traditional Career Path Model. When issues pertaining to career politics arise, today's workforce prefers direct answers–straight talk.

The Tail Wagging the Dog

This phenomenon occurs when executives avoid frank discussion about the politics of promotion.

Leaders must take affirmative steps to maintain credibility by practicing openness and keeping pace with the changes occurring in the workforce. Side-stepping issues of promotion politics reflects badly on management's assertions that employees are the most highly valued members of the organization.

Weak Point #2
The Traditional Career Path Model Fosters a False Sense of Security by Promoting Intellectualization

Fear not those who argue, fear those who dodge.
Marie Von Eschenbach

Under the influence of intellectualization, an executive may lapse into a psychological defense mechanism, which operates below the level of full conscious awareness. Intellectualization is a coping style that prevents a person from doing deep introspective thinking that might cause him or her to see things as they actually exist. To everyone's astonishment, the executive may hide his or her true feelings by using well measured words in the hope of appeasing people and creating the effect of fairness. As a defense mechanism, intellectualization protects executives from unpleasant thoughts and experiences. In-depth self-analysis may be threatening to many executives. By not facing their fears executives remain in denial.

Playing Dodge Ball With Reality

This is the intellectual equivalent of faking head moves, ducking or jump over unpleasant topics.

Anxieties and stress about possible confrontations may cause executives to speak about distasteful subjects like promotion politics in a detached and impersonal way. Because of this, an executive's reflective reasoning is not what it should be. Thus, an executive may not be fully cognizant of how his or her reaction to topics like promotion politics is coming across. At another level, executives may use highly abstract concepts, restricting their comments to purely theoretical speculation about whether promotions politics even exist. The above efforts to intellectualize problems away affords executives a way to temporarily avoid addressing difficult issues, which will eventually come back to haunt them.

Weak Point #2

The Traditional Career Path Model Fosters a False Sense of Security by Promoting Intellectualizing

We're all hustlers;
we're all as honest as we can afford to be.
Lenny Bruce

Take for example the notion of reform, which seems to be a favorite term among some CEOs. When the boss is in full executive mode he or she may speak in highly idealistic terms about reforming the organization's promotion practices. Yet, when it comes to actual progress, little has been done. Changes may be cosmetic and limited to small, token, incremental steps. Thus, 100% reform of the organization's promotion practices exists largely as a conceptual idea.

Is the word *reform* intellectual code talk for:

- **Buying time until the next CEO comes along and inherits the problem.**

- **Stalling by saying "Just be patient." You can't rush things. These things take time.**

- **Finding a scapegoat to blame. Confusing the issue by passing the buck between executives.**

Executives mean well, but they wind up force feeding regurgitated pabulum to people by always asserting that promotions are won through hard work and not politics when in reality it may be the other way around.

Weak Point #2
The Traditional Career Path Model Fosters a False Sense of Security by Promoting Intellectualizing

Einstein's theory of relativity, as practiced by congressmen,
simply means getting members of your family on the payroll.
James H. Boren

Unless there is a respectful relationship between people, their emotions tend to interfere and make them feel uncomfortable when talking about career politics. If the subject of advancement is perceived as a "hot potato," superiors prefer to keep their subordinates at arm's length. This causes bosses to take a cerebral and linear approach to explaining how people advance in their organization.

Don't Ask and Don't Tell

In organizations where the fear factor is high, the words "full disclosure" and "promotion practices" cannot be used in the same sentence.

For example, management may generalize and stress that the organization values employees and has a mission statement and business ethics. By deflecting the conversation in this manner, managers hope that these assertions will suffice for a candid discussion about career politics. If pressed to address the topic of career advancement politics, some executives tend to play down the idea and assure staff that it is not as bad as it used to be, and lastly they may resort to making glowing comments about reforming the promotion practices.

The mass of men lead lives of quiet desperation.
Henry David Thoreau

Weak Point #2
The Traditional Career Path Model
Fosters a False Sense of
Security by Promoting Intellectualizing

Many of the obstacles for change which have been attributed to human nature are in fact due to the inertia of institutions and the voluntary desire of powerful classes to maintain the existing status.
John Dewey

The defense mechanism of intellectualization is symptomatic of people who are uncomfortable when they have to think outside the box of conventional wisdom. Minimizing the existence of promotion politics only adds fuel to the problems that already exists. Reciting the virtues and seemingly scripted opinions about the Traditional Career Path Model makes many bosses and staff seem impervious to the realities of the workplace or, worse, that they suffer from selective honesty. Consequently, this level of denial precludes any ongoing constructive discussions about:

Ageism	Discrimination towards people over age 40 Treatment based on class vs. individual merit
Careerism	Doing what ever it takes to get the position you want and safeguarding it
Favoritism*	Showing more kindness and indulgence to some person or persons than to others
Homophobia	Irrational fear of gay and lesbian lifestyles
Nepotism*	Appointing relatives to desirable positions
Racism*	Discrimination, persecution, and domination based on feelings that one ethnic group is superior to another
Sexism	Discrimination based on gender

* Webster's Dictionary

Weak Point #3
The Traditional Career Path Model
Represents a Great Theory, but Flawed Reality

All political questions, all matters of right,
are at bottom, only questions of might. August Bebel

Upon close examination, it seems that the Traditional Career Path Model is part fact and part fiction. Under highly ideal conditions, it presents a well-reasoned approach to advancement. Executives always cast themselves and the Traditional Career Path model in a favorable light. Management describes it as worker friendly, but the advantages of the model (power and control) tend to favor managers who sometimes exploit staff who are unfamiliar with the ways that promotions are handled.

Slippery Slope

The model is composed of bromides that are hard to debunk, especially when presented by higher-ups whom employees are fearful of alienating with challenging questions.

Fictionally speaking, the model has a fairy-tale quality that conveys the feeling that "only the pure-of-heart succeed." Historically, the purpose of folk tales is to relay messages about character building and about life's dos and don'ts for survival. They spark off a lot of feel-good sensations that belie the truth.

It's All In The Playing

The values of character building presented in childhood fables are honorable; however, the real world of career advancement plays by rules that are part fictitious and part true as gospel.

Seen in this light, The Traditional Career Path Model is the perfect myth. It is applied generously in an effort to explain how promotions are bestowed upon persons deemed to be the most qualified.

Weak Point #4
The Traditional Career Path Model
Shows that
Form Does Not Follow Function

As far as the laws of mathematics refer to reality, they are not certain,
and as far as they are certain, they do not refer to reality.
Albert Einstein

The model reflects a "one size fits all" approach to career advancement. Outwardly, it appears very straight forward. Inwardly, it is a sophisticated behavioral modification process. The form that it takes is to plant the idea that if certain career steps are followed promotions will come one's way. As positive as the initial four steps are (Education, Hard Work, Team Player, Cooperate with the Boss), it is the final step (Best Qualified Person Is Promoted) that makes people feel that, functionally, the model is not all that it's cracked up to be. In the end, form and function go their separate ways.

The Hypnotized Never Lie

On a functional level it might appear that the Traditional Career Path Model is a dreadful failure. But, ideologically it succeeds by instilling a behavioral modification process that the organization needs in order to ensure that people toe the organization party line.

The carrot that leads people down The Traditional Career Path is always in the eye of the beholder who senses that an executive slot is close at hand. Your advancement is in the hands of the boss who does a good job of talking up the hopes of promoting people, but never fully satisfies their need--that is unless you have met the X Factor requirement. This brings to the fore that career advancement is part public relations gimmick and part reality.

Career Shaping Questions

1. **Complete the following sentence by circling *A, B*, or *C*.**

   People get promoted on the basis of:

   A. **Hard work plus who you know and who knows you.**

   B. **Hard work, merit, and virtues.**

   C. **Other**_____

   Explain _____

2. **To what extent do you think that the Traditional Career Path Model is the perfect myth for controlling career advancement and perpetuating the idea that promotions are always fair - based on merit?**

   Circle your choice.

1	2	3	4	5	6	7	8	9	10
Disagree with statement									**Agree with statement**

   Explain _____

Career Shaping Questions

3. **When it comes to the Politics of Promotion, how would you describe today's employees?**

   Circle your choice.

   Not Politically   1   2   3   4   5   6   7   8   9   10   **Extremely**
   Inclined   **Political**

   Explain _____

4. **When it comes to the Politics of Promotion, how politically inclined are you? Circle your choice.**

   Not Politically   1   2   3   4   5   6   7   8   9   10   **Extremely**
   Inclined   **Political**

   Explain _____

5. **Simply having a college degree(s), certificate, or license will get you promoted to the top levels in your organization.**

   Mark your choice: Yes_____   No_____

   If yes, give an example of how this applies in real life.

   _____

   If no, what else does a person need in order to get to the top?

   _____

Chapter 4

Content Of Character: A Model for Career Advancement

*In talking with successful CEOs of large companies, I hear
one recurrent theme: "the willingness to pay the price."
This phrase implies an intense motivation, a burning desire to
become chief executive. The price includes not just consistently
long hours, and longer days, but grueling travel schedules,
emotional stress, loss of privacy, putting one's reputation on the
line, guilt for the neglect of spouses and children, and little time,
if any, left over for oneself.*   Thomas R. Horton
President and CEO,
American Management Association

Moving Up By Stepping On People

But, when I get to the top I will have ethics.

Content of Character
A Model for Career Advancement

*Character is determined more by the lack of certain experiences
than by those one has had.*   *Friedrich Nietzche*

Content of Character Ideology

Work hard
Stand in line
Pay your dues
Play by the rules
Don't be a complainer
Wait your turn and you will
be discovered and promoted

Lorenzo Flores

As a true piece of Americana, the Content of Character Model has achieved a place of prominence in the workplace, for two reasons:

1. It gives people hope that by sheer determination they can rise above all the obstacles. If they don't advance, they can be philosophical about it and say that "in the end everything works out for the best," or "that it just wasn't meant to be." Although this model is controlled by management, it carries the inherent wish and belief among some staff that the organization's promotion process is designed to be fair, balanced, and perhaps, even divinely inspired.

2. It allows the hiring officials to enjoy their infallible prerogative of saying who they feel is a quality person. Executives like to say they are good judges of talent and instinctively know when a candidate for a position has "it" or, as they say, the "wow factor." In the end, it seems that only the selecting official knows what he or she means by Content of Character.

Content of Character
A
Model for Career Advancement

*All cartoon characters and fables must be exaggeration caricatures.
It is the very nature of fantasy and fable.*   **Walt Disney**

In the World of Career Advancement Politics
Content of Character refers to:

**The sum total of traits that management chooses to
play up or play down in order to make a person
appear promotion worthy.**

Example _____

In this model, it is believed that good clean living and righteous
moral fiber provide the extra lift that moves people to the top. This
is the cherished belief that anyone with the correct motivation,
outlook, and discipline can become a CEO.

Proponents of this model say these traits are available to everyone;
it's a matter of taking responsibility for one's career and not seeing
oneself as a victim. In other words, people who cannot make it to the
top on their own, like a lot of executives claim they did, suffer from a
character weakness. Staunch supporters of the Content of Character
Model throw out words like "competence" and "hard work" but fail
to seriously analyze the role that "good old boy/gal" politics played
in their career moves. Good "old boy" clubby politics refers to the
"quid pro quo" of you do this for me and I will do this for you. And
through this mutual "back scratching" we will promote each other
up the ladder of success. Translation: Protect the private club by
keeping things quiet and low profile.

How Some Executives Use and Abuse the Content of Character Model

Reputation is character minus what you've been caught doing.
M. Lapoce

Executives with a Machiavellian bent know that they must distance themselves from the organization's informal promotion practices. This empowers them to appear objective and politically ethical. Below is a description of how this is done.

Staying Neutral

When it comes to career advancement, management likes to say that it does not play favorites, that no matter what, it remains impartial and detached from the promotion process. Prudent executives like to say that upward mobility takes place when an individual takes control of his or her career development. It's not the responsibility of the organization to "hand things to people." Promotion has to be earned.

Political Correctness

Where has all the truth in advertising gone? History shows that politically driven organizations will always position themselves as being socially responsible, innovative, and free from the taint of shady politics.

Truth in Career Advancement

By identifying itself as an Equal Opportunity Employer, an organization professes to have unbiased promotion practices, e.g., there is no informal shadow organization.

Neither skin color, age, life style, or disability are factors that impact management's decisions on whom to move up to the top echelons. This conveys the message that the Content of Character Model is a picture of honesty and does not tolerate people currying favor through "political games." This is what organizations say for public consumption.

Content of Character Model
Weak Points

Every man has three characters-that which he exhibits, that
which he has, and that which he thinks he has. Alphonse Karr

Proponents of this dearly loved but under analyzed model missed an excellent opportunity to construct a great theory. Instead, they put forth an abstract construct that is extremely slippery. By failing to present a balanced perspective on what it takes to become a top manager, the theory takes on a synthetic-like quality.

Who Says You Don't Have the Right Stuff

Raising or lowering the bar for advancement seems to have more to do with management's perceptions and needs than with the true character of the individual selected for the position.

Can Content of Character be used as a smoke screen to hide secret X Factor preferences? Unfortunately, many organizations have strayed away from the actual intent of the phrase "content of character." The model concentrates so heavily on putting responsibility on the individual to develop character that it is easy to overlook the role that management plays in selecting and promoting people it perceives as the most desirable. Thus, it is not unusual for organizations to not hire a person even though he or she has the necessary technical skills and background qualifications. Generally, for reasons known only to them, decision makers feel that the candidate is not a good fit with the organization's culture. But for the political comfort zone factor, the organization could have hired the individual on a probationary status and helped him or her learn to do the job according to the organization's style and needs. When hiring or promoting people, management must consider the adage that says: Hire for potential and train for skill. This way Equal Employment Opportunity becomes a true executive career advancement ladder.

Weak Point #1
Content of Character Model
Downplays the Idea
of
Promotion Politics

The most successful managers are those that can quickly grasp how their bosses think.   Amy Bermar

The Content of Character Model tends to cancel itself out due to the fact that it fails to recognize the impact that politics has on careers. Career politics intensifies in direct proportion to the status, power, and salary of the position being sought.

**Study the contradictions
that make up career advancement.**

By not discussing career advancement politics you are contributing to the problem; you are enabling the status quo to go unchallenged. Ongoing progressive discussions are essential to change.

No More Mr. Nice Guy

Unless leaders can grapple with career advancement issues that affect the workplace, they themselves will fall victim to the politics of promotion.

The best way to not fall victim to the politics of promotion is to bring it out of the closet and talk about it. This steals its thunder and breaks the spell it has over people. Politics is a way of coping, surviving, and even thriving in organizations. Not recognizing this creates a distorted view of the organization. Eventually, the downplaying of career politics results in feelings of betrayal of people who are "in the trenches" and struggling to move up. Even the most principled person recognizes that people who ignore the politics of promotion do so at their own peril. The remedy is to ask questions while keeping one eye on your career goals and the other eye on the organization's practices.

Weak Point #2
The Content of Character Model
Stresses that People Make it on Their Own

What I lack in know-how,
I more than make up for in know-who. Mal Hancock

The model skims over the fact that professional contacts and personal relationships are pivotal to forming psychological contracts, which lead to success. Besides diligent work, advancement requires a mindset of reciprocity between those who aspire to move up and those already there. Advancement opportunities are conferred upon people whom management deems as having "high potential." This is seen as spending resources on people who will bring the biggest return on investment (ROI).

Summary

Many a man's reputation would not know his character
if they met on the street. Elbert Hubbard

Character counts, especially when one knows what attributes management is counting. This view likens the process of assessing the Content of Character to a two-way street. An organization has the right and duty to learn about a candidate's background. On the same level of importance, an organization's character must also be scrutinized in terms of its past and present promotion practices.

Executive Double Speak

Understanding management's collective character and promotion practices is important because it is hard to detect how the phrase "Content of Character" is being used.

Summary

*In selection the emphasis is on rejection. The purpose is to
select from a large group of applicants the person best suited for
a particular role. In placement, however, the emphasis is on how
a particular individual can best be used. Henry L. Tosi*

Even the slightest hint of a character blemish can be used as a pretext
for disqualifying a person. In most organizations, the decision as to
whether a person has the right character for a promotion is left up
to the hiring officials—whose jobs depends on their following the
agenda set by the top brass.

It's a Tough Job, But Somebody Has To Do It

**From management's standpoint, assessing Content
Of Character and who to promote to the top becomes a
strenuous task of deciding which character traits
to accentuate and which to minimize.**

That's Why Executives Get Paid The Big Bucks

Are you a maverick or are you malleable? The truth is executives
want "malleable mavericks" who come to heel when told to do
so. Organizations seem to want people whose values and ethics
are not so rigid that there is no room for the organization's way of
doing things. While the ideals of the Content of Character Model
are highly praised, it is unlikely that a person who is totally honest
would make it very far in today's workplace. Could it be that too
much honesty makes a person appear to be vulnerable, naive, and
a potential whistle blower? And this does not sit right with people
who feel that flexibility is the key to survival in an organization.
Perhaps there is some truth to the idea that in order to get along with
people, we need to (within reason) overlook their negative traits and
focus on their positive traits. Flawed people working in an imperfect
organization can, with the right guidance, correct their problems and
help maintain a healthier workplace environment.

Summary

If you are mediocre and you grovel, you shall succeed. Pierre de Beaumarchais

"Nice guys always finish first." This comforting message and its implied virtues of integrity and unselfishness make up the belief system of this endearing model. It seems that management on one hand advocates this model, while with the other hand it manipulates the model. In this fashion, management can make a person's career, break a person's career, or marginalize a person. In the end, it seems that the search for the ideal applicant comes down to the following lopsided equation. The best fit for the organization is arrived at by adding up management's professional and personal needs and subdividing them by the positive and negative attributes of the candidate that closely match what the ideal applicant would possess. On the surface this process appears 100% objective, but below the surface it allows higher-ups to be sufficiently subjective in hiring people who possess the professional and personal traits they want in a "dream worker." The person who comes closest to matching management's ideals is selected and declared the "best fit" for the organization.

Hiring the Dream Team

Management's Professional Needs + Management's Personal Needs   = Best Fit
Candidate Closely Matching Management's Flight of Fancy

Real world wisdom holds that in order to be promoted, a person must match management's agenda, or at least the greater part of it. Since management controls the promotion process and practices, it determines if there is a good character fit between the organization and the worker.

The Dynamics of Career Advancement

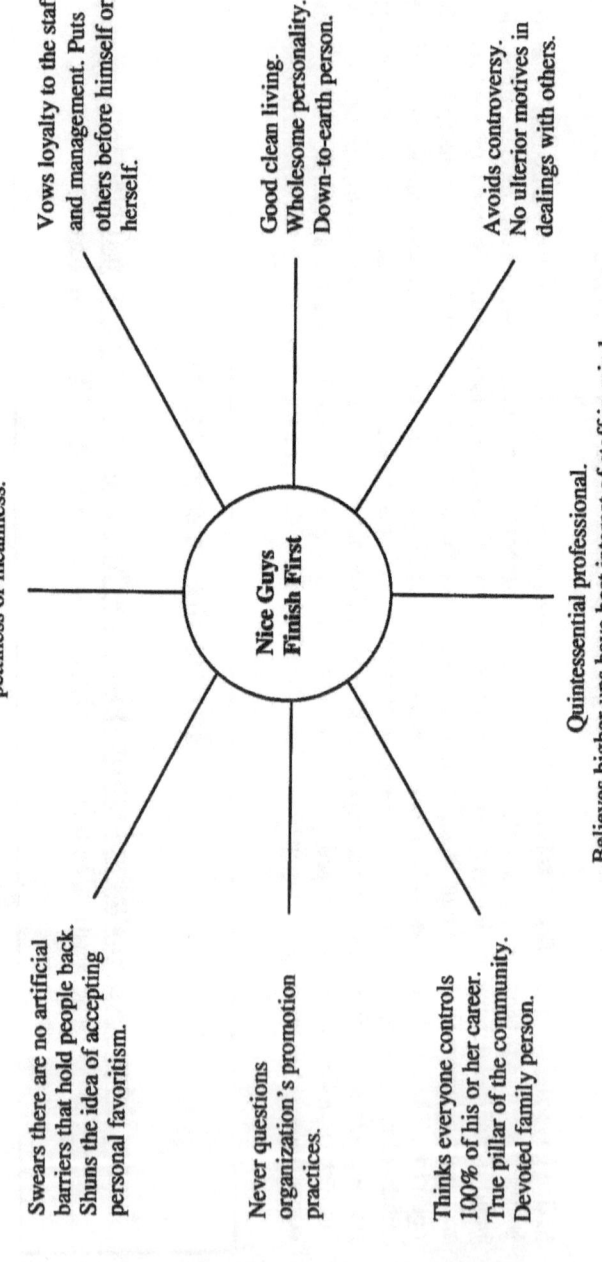

Content Of Character Model For Career Advancement

Nice Guys
Finish First

Magnanimous personality – Noble in word and deed. Rises above pettiness or meanness.

Vows loyalty to the staff and management. Puts others before himself or herself.

Good clean living. Wholesome personality. Down-to-earth person.

Avoids controversy. No ulterior motives in dealings with others.

Quintessential professional. Believes higher-ups have best interest of staff in mind.

Thinks everyone controls 100% of his or her career. True pillar of the community. Devoted family person.

Never questions organization's promotion practices.

Swears there are no artificial barriers that hold people back. Shuns the idea of accepting personal favoritism.

Career Shaping Questions

1. **In the search for the ideal candidate management seems to prefer certain formal and informal traits in the people it promotes. Can you identify these attributes?**

<table>
<tr><td colspan="2">Formal traits
On the record</td><td colspan="2">Informal traits
Off the record</td></tr>
<tr><td>_____</td><td>_____</td><td>_____</td><td>_____</td></tr>
<tr><td>_____</td><td>_____</td><td>_____</td><td>_____</td></tr>
<tr><td>_____</td><td>_____</td><td>_____</td><td>_____</td></tr>
</table>

The Best Candidate
Using the above lists, identify the two formal and two informal traits
that represent management's key preferences

_____	_____
_____	_____

2. **How do people who bent the rules and got promoted justify enforcing the same rules they bent while working and politicking their way up the career ladder?**

   Explain _____

Career Shaping Questions

3. Complete the following sentence by selecting *A* or *B*.

   In career advancement nice guys always finish...

   A. last _____   *B.* first _____

   Explain: _____

4. How do you define the phrase "bending the rules?"

   _____

   How does your boss define the phrase "bending the rules?"

   _____

5. How do you feel about people who bend the rules to get the job done and get promoted?

   Circle your choice.

   Oppose 1   2   3   4   5   6   7   8   9   10 Tolerate

6. Why do some higher-ups tolerate bending the rules? From the list below write in your number 1, 2, 3 choices.

   _____ Up-and-coming executives are expected to have this ability.

   _____ It's an informal trait expected in all executives.

   _____ Management wants to know how creative prospective executives can be when it comes to beating competitors.

   _____ Its an unspoken executive test to see who fits into their comfort zone and the organization's culture.

   _____ Other_____

Career Shaping Questions

7. **To what degree would you bend the rules to get promoted? Circle your choice.**

   Never   1   2   3   4   5   6   7   8   9   1 0   Always

   Explain _____

8. **How do you define the word gamesmanship?**

   _____

   How does your boss define the word gamesmanship?

   _____

9. **To what extent could your differences with the boss about gamesmanship* impact your career advancement?**

   None   1   2   3   4   5   6   7   8   9   1 0   High impact

   Explain _____

Gamesmanship* A competitive mindset that utilizes the best of human nature and the worst of human nature. The intent is to gain strategic advantages over others. This is done by staying on top of your game, but finding ways to throw competitors off of their game plans. Shrewd gamers win by stretching the rules as far as management permits. Their worse fear is losing the competitive advantage. A hard core gamesman avoids a fair fight. If he or she finds themselves in a fair fight they feel it's because they did not prepare themselves better. These are people on their way to the top and they know how to get it done.

Chapter 5

The Sports Model
for
Career Advancement

Career Advancement is not a spectator sport.
It is a full contact sport,
it can physically kick your butt,
ethically challenge you,
emotionally drain you,
financially pressure you,
mentally block you and
intellectually punish you.
This makes Career Advancement the quintessential blood sport.
Lorenzo Flores

Develop the Killer Instinct

The quarterback executive puts it all on the line.
He sees himself as a man of action who finds
and exploits the other team's weakness.

Not winning is the biggest fear
Winning must be in your DNA
Losing is not an option

The Sports Model for Career Advancement

The idea in this game isn't to win popularity polls or to be a good guy to everyone. The name of the game is to win.   Bill Martin

Of the three Conventional Wisdom Models, the sports analogy model is the most captivating because it expresses the ideal that competition brings out the very best in everyone. It likens career advancement to rough and tumble competitive sports. It's the great American pastimes of baseball, football, tennis, golf, basketball, auto racing, hunting, fishing, and mountain climbing all rolled into the struggle for career advancement. On another level, metaphorically speaking, sports lingo is used to describe all that is determined to be good by management and staff. The notion of true sportsmanship and taking home the prize has a down-to-earth appeal. No one wants to be a bad sport, everyone wants to be a good sport who abides by the rules of the game and never complains.

Play Like a Champion

This action-filled model is used by managers, who try to motivate workers by running their organization like a professional sports team.

Put me in, coach, I'm ready to play. The manager assumes the role of the coach who "calls the shots" and "drills the team" to a competitive edge. Like coaches of a team going to the Super Bowl or the World Series, they claim to recruit only the most qualified people to fill key positions. Unfortunately, many coaches prefer outstanding game players over players with outstanding ethical standards. Since the goal is to win, managers can do as they please in terms of deciding who will be hired, trained, and promoted. The same goes for deciding who will be the back benchers. With this in mind, the Sports Model is based on the following points:

Teamwork
Human Sacrifice
Symbolism and Pageantry

Competition Brings Out The Best In People

1. Teamwork

Some management groups are not good at problem-solving and decision-making precisely because the participants have weak egos and are uncomfortable with competition. Chris Argyris

"Stay on top of your game" is the frequently heard mantra of managers, coaches, and players who receive an adrenalin rush from the thrill of dominating opponents. Sports stories and sports hype are used to create a desire to be #1. Individuals are disciplined to subordinate their needs and desires in order to focus on the game and nothing else. In order to win, team players must put aside their egos and cooperate with one another so as to achieve the organization's goals. After all, everyone loves a winner and everyone wants to be on a winning team--we're in the business of winning.

2. Human Sacrifice

In the fight for survival, a tie or split decision simply will not do.
Merle L. Meacham

We're not playing for a tie. The trick to winning is to get pumped up and stay pumped up. Some players live and die by the scoreboard of super human achievements. When it comes to making contributions, nothing replaces personal risk-taking and delivering the right performance. The idea of offering up one's life to the organization in return for the privilege of pursuing a career may cause people to become workaholics or place their health in jeopardy. For all practical purposes, they have become extensions of the organization. Their home may serve as a satellite office for the organization. Superstar athletes are held up as role models to illustrate how they overcame adversity to "get back into the game" and give a 110% effort. It's not whether you win or lose; it's how passionately you play the game that counts. In other words, do it for the game. This love of the game helps people transcend personal problems, illness, or injury. Continuing to play becomes a badge of honor in the game of oneupsmanship. This shows just how addictive playing the career advancement game can be.

2. Human Sacrifice

High positions must be fought for inch by inch,
and held by a vigilance that never sleeps. Elbert Hubbard

Expressions like "we're going to the mat on this one" or "the ball is in his court" attempt to infuse the everyday working person with a combat sports mentality. The ideal of a clean, wholesome rivalry has a tremendous hold on the American psyche. People who passionately believe in the sports model fancy themselves as being on the "All Star Team." According to the followers of this model, the final score and the statistics tell it all.

You Don't Win Second Place, You Lose First Place

Clearly defined winners and losers make sports the perfect metaphor for organizations that have a passion for success and a zeal for defeating competitors.

---

3. Symbolism and Pageantry

In life, as in a football game, the principle to follow is:
Hit the line hard.   *Theodore Roosevelt*

Locked and dialed into winning. Winning attitudes are conveyed through pithy slogans, enthusiastic flag waving, championship banners, imposing emblems, and catchy theme songs. Some people find cheerleading and doing the human wave at company conferences exhilarating. Others feel that graphic jargon like "slam dunk" excites and inspires sports aficionados. Victory celebrations with ticker tape parades, champagne, and trophies whet the appetite of people who compete to be the organization's MVP (Most Valuable Player). Careerists intuitively know that active participation in these activities is not optional; it is mandatory, even if not publicly stated. For that matter, so is understanding the history behind the pomp and symbols cherished by the organization leaders.

The Workplace is not a Sports Arena

Nice guys finish last. Leo Durocher

A come-from-behind win is a sweet thing. In order to squeeze the most work out of employees, organizations, in the name of motivating staff, find clever ways to blur the line between being an athlete and being an employee. Frankly, some organizations prefer a blurred reality. Below are concepts used by some organizations to create a hazy mental mist between the roles of employees and superstar athletes.

Superstar Athlete	Employee Of The Year
Hall of Fame	Wall of Fame
Number of games played	Years of dependable service
Career batting average	Career profits-Top Producer
Tackles and interceptions	Preventing losses and saving money
Runs scored or yardage gained	Correct decisions made under pressure
Hits at bat	Proposals adopted by the organization
Home runs or touchdowns	Major projects completed
Pinch hitter or field goals kicked	Number of times one assisted boss with projects-saved boss's reputation
Stolen bases or causing opponent to commit mental errors	Master the exceptions to every rule and use them to outscore competitors
Number of times participated in Super Bowls or World Series games	Engaging in major competition against opponents. Close profitable deals. Mr. Touchdown
Number of times named to All Star Games or Pro-Bowls	On the boss's special team. Number of times selected for high profile projects. Mr. Double Play
Awards, trophies, rings	Lapel pins, plaques, bonus, perks
Endorsement contracts for product advertising	Letters of commendation. Clients request employee by name

How the Sports Model Fails in the Workplace

Whoever said, "It's not whether you win or lose that counts,"
probably lost.   Martina Navratilova

Step up to the plate and bring your "A" game. Turning career advancement into a sport has tremendous appeal, but it does not capture the essence of the daily grind that occurs in the workplace. The following five points show how the model misguides people when it comes to the politics of promotion.

1

Sports Have Impartial Referees; Organizations Don't

We've got to find a way to win. I'm willing to start cheating.
New England tight end Marv Cook

It takes what it takes to win. Don't hesitate to give the other guy hell. If you hesitate you lose.Unsportsmanlike conduct in "the pros" is monitored by a neutral third party in charge of enforcing the rules. When a violation occurs, the referees can stop the game and do an instant replay of the infraction. The perpetrators may be ejected from the game or subjected to a monetary fine.

Political Football

Organizations shun the idea of an independent third-party referee. They are convinced that they can resolve internal problems on their own.

Biting an opponents ear is not a good thing. At least in professional sports there are certain moves or physical holds on opponents that are banned because they are dangerous. But, in career advancement, figuratively speaking, there seems to be an anything-goes attitude - no holds barred. Often, in workplace situations, the organization's managers are too close to the situation to be objective. Very likely they're part of the problem themselves—they are predisposed to sweep things under the rug. Only when they are forced to bring in an outside reviewer do they acknowledge the need for intervention or change.

How the Sports Model Fails in the Workplace

I want this team to win, I'm obsessed with winning, with discipline, with achieving. That's what this country's all about.

George Steinbrenner

2

Denies the Duality of Organizational Behavior

Show me a good sportsman, and I'll show you a player I'm looking to trade.

Leo Durocher

By presenting only the positive side of sports and career advancement, organizations do themselves and staff a disservice. Always painting a chaste picture of what it takes to advance or dancing around issues related to the politics of advancement creates resentment among employees. The statement "he or she won't play ball with us" usually refers to the fact that a person is not willing to play by the rules set by the other team. Not going along with the informal game plan may impact a person's career.

Don't Be Distracted by Cheerleading Side Shows

Employees are ahead of management when it comes to knowing that a motivational speech delivered by a celebrity is not equal to one that addresses the dynamics of career advancement politics.

In order to get people motivated to "get with the program," organizations may resort to bringing in famous sports figures to sign autographs, discuss teamwork, and talk about their glory days on the tennis court, gridiron, basketball court, or baseball diamond. Having a sports figure talk about leadership is supposed to in someway substitute for a frank question and answer discussion regarding the politics of promotion. Contrary to management's thinking, the staff knows that this does not do the trick. Today's employees have a keen sense of career advancement and want information that prepares them to assume high-level positions.

How the Sports Model Fails in the Workplace

Football combines the two worst features of American life.
It is violence punctuated by committee meetings.   George Will

3

Fosters a Gladiator Mindset

I'd walk through hell in a gasoline suit to play baseball. Pete Rose

Don't hold back! Give it all you've got. Sometimes doing things that are injurious to one's health, e.g., enduring stress and pain, is seen as a part of the price to be paid for success. This may amount to giving the organization your best physical and mental health years. It's as if the organization is saying, "If you're not injured, you're not living up to your potential." It is expected that you will make a name for yourself by breaking records, raising the bar, and setting new standards. Some organizations believe that unless a worker is always on the edge of burn-out, or feels highly pressured, he or she is not doing all he or she can for the organization.

The Quick and the Dead-Ended

There are those who are always ready, willing, and able to do whatever it takes to beat rivals.

Game on! Just like in hard hitting, smash-mouth competitive sports, injuries and casualties are expected and tolerated as part of the game. Some people actually believe the word *dedicated* is spelled dead-icated.   This has its counterpart in competition for advancement, where people suffer work injuries or even die at their desk--the tomb of the unknown executive. Unfortunately, before the corpse is cold co-workers are fighting and picking over his or her office supplies and parking space. In a seemingly compassionate voice a former political rival of the deceased may say, "I know she would want me to have her job." In other words, human sacrifice on the high altar of the organization is the ultimate price that some pay for advancement. Greater love has no man or woman than to give his or her life for the grand and glorious cause of the organization.

How the Sports Model Fails in the Workplace

I do not think that winning is the most important thing.
I think winning is the only thing. Bill Veeck

4

Sports Builds Character and Teaches Cheating

Sports do not build character, they reveal it. Heywood Brown

No one likes to lose! A coach can teach people to play by the rules as well as how to bend the rules. Finding ways to reinterpret the official regulations, or learning how to get an opposing player to commit an error, is the fine art of strategizing. Professional sports are filled with examples of athletes "getting away" with breaking the rules when the referee is not looking. This has its direct counterpart in the workplace when rules are broken in order to expedite a project or promotion. If you are not cheating you are not trying hard enough.

A Long Standing Tradition of Cheating

The unique paradox of a sporting character is that one must respect his or her opponents, but at the same time find clever ways to break their spirit, undermine their confidence, and scare the hell out of them.

As some coaches say, in order to win you have to take risks and be hungrier than the other guy. Even when you're winning, play like you're behind. The fear of losing may drive some people to use an assortment of "gamesmanship" tactics. In the workplace, this amounts to keeping score of peer rivals' successes and failures. Some players may even overtly or covertly sabotage a competitor's game plan. The statement "knowing the score" seems to say it all. This is code talk for knowing on and off the record how the other guy is doing. This allows opposing players to devise new strategies to gain the winning edge. Failure is not an option.

Why the Sports Model Fails in the Workplace

There's only two kinds of coaches;
them that's been fired and them that's about to be fired.
Bum Phillips

5

Assuming That All Employees Are Sports Fans

If winning isn't important, why do they keep score? Adolph Rupp

A major league moment for the record books. Great game plays and sports statistics are not part of everyone's standard jargon and way of thinking. Employees who do not share the boss's exuberance for the "big play" of the week could be overlooked for promotions. A lack of excitement for the boss's favorite sport or hobby or ignorance of the names and salaries of sports heros might be perceived as an unwillingness to socialize. To some people a sports game is bigger than life and reinforces the notion that only the strong survive.

Monday Morning Quarterbacking

Gamesmanship statements such as
"making points with the boss"
and
"putting points on the score board"
have their roots in jock talk.

"The gloves are coming off." Sports mania, with its push-and-shove tactics, may be a "turn-off" to employees who are not sports enthusiasts or are not motivated by the need to "settle an old score." Some managers need to realize that being a "sports jock" is no guarantee that a person will be a competent executive. It may be just the opposite perspective that is needed to make fair and important decisions.

Summary

Being in politics is like being a football coach.
You have to be smart enough to understand the game
and dumb enough to think it's important. Eugene McCarthy

Competition breeds politics. Supporters of the Sports Model for Career Advancement believe that to win you must want it more than the other guy. To make your mark you must dominate or crush the competition. Many people want to be hailed as courageous champions and gallant conquering heros. The sports analogy model makes literal sense for this take-no-prisoners mentality. In a twisted sort of way, it can be a morale booster. Another school of thought is that the Sports Model is very beguiling and trivializes career advancement issues by not taking matters more seriously.

You Always Have to Be Looking Over Your Shoulder
and
Listening for Foot Steps

Unlike sports games, which have time-outs and referees, career advancement is a twenty-four-hour-a-day job with a seemingly no-holds-barred attitude.

Example _____

Overall, the concept has high situational value, but should never be used as the primary model for career advancement. It must be tempered with the knowledge that few valid comparisons can be drawn between highly overpaid professional sports figures and the daily political routines that people contend with at work. Unfortunately, even sports heros confess that they are not good role models for kids or adults.

Overview of the Sports Model:
The Good, the Bad, and the Nasty

The game of life is a lot like football. You have to tackle your problems,
block your fears, and score points when you get the opportunity.
Lewis Gizzard

Winning is Job #1

Ideals of Sports Model	Realities of Sports Model
Competition brings out the best in people	Sports builds character and teaches cheating
Symbolism and pageantry Everything is a ritual	The Sports Model denies the duality of (good and bad) organizational behavior
Teamwork "Win one for the Gipper."	The Sports Model fosters a gladiator mindset. Be prepared to give your all for the organization's survival
Self-sacrifice "Take one for the team."	Sports have impartial referees; organizations don't.
Individual effort "Hit one out of the ballpark."	Sports Model automatically assumes all employees are sports fans

158

Sports Jargon Used In The Workplace

In America it is sports that is the opiate of the masses. Russell Baker

Football
Touchdown
Performance-enhancing drugs
Hail Mary Pass
Tackle
Quarterback sneak
Goal line
Block
Long bomb
Trick play

Boxing
Knock-out punch
Low blow
On the ropes
Land an uppercut
Roll with the punches
Throw in the towel
Heavy weight
Head butt
Left hook

Motor Sports
Shifting gears
Pit crew
Lap the competition
Illegal equipment
In the driver's seat
Spin-out
Victory lap
Winner's circle
Checkered flag

Baseball
Home run
Stolen base
100 MPH fast ball
Strike out
On steroids
Hard ball
Strike three
Use a corked bat
Heavy hitter

Basketball
Slam dunk
Full court press
Foul out
Time out
Time clock
Double team
Turn around jump shot
Out of bounds
Cheap shot
Sell the bump

Golf
Hole in one
Handicap
Chip shot
Par for the course
Go the distance
Alter the score
Sand trap
Country Club

Career Shaping Questions

1. **Select from (*A* or *B*) the word that you feel best completes the following sentence.**

   Competition brings out the...

   A. **worst in people** _____

   B. **best in people** _____

   Explain _____

2. **How important is winning in your organization, department, unit?**

   Circle your choice.

1	2	3	4	5	6	7	8	9	10

   Winning is   **Winning**
   not important   **is everything**

   Explain _____

3. **How do you get pumped up (mental and physical preparation) in order to preform your best at work?**

   Explain _____

Career Shaping Questions

4. How does your boss get pumped up (mental and physical preparation) in order to perform his or her best at work?

Explain _____

5. Higher-ups and co-workers sometimes use sports cliches to describe their work situations. List the sports expressions or sayings heard in your workplace.

_____

_____

6. If your boss played sports, what level did he or she play at and what position did he or she play?

High School Sport(s) _____ Position(s) played _____

College Sport(s) _____ Position(s) played _____

Professional Sport(s) _____ Position(s) played _____

Career Shaping Questions

7. **Sports**
   List the boss's favorite sports   **List your favorite sports**

   _____ _____   _____ _____

8. **List sports interests you and the boss have in common**

   _____ _____   _____ _____

9. **Competition breeds politics. How true is this when it comes to career advancement to the top?**

   1   2   3   4   5   6   7   8   9   10
   No, competition   Yes, competition
   does not breed politics   breeds politics

   Explain _____

10. **Is your organization a true meritocracy or a political meritocracy?**

    True meritocracy--100% free of bias and politics. Promotions are based on ability or achievement.

    Political meritocracy--politics count.   Promotions are based on talents, abilities, connections, achievements, and appearances as defined by higher-ups.

    Rank your organization. Circle your choice.

    1   2   3   4   5   6   7   8   9   10
    True   Political
    meritocracy   meritocracy

Career Shaping Questions

11. What do you think appeals to your boss about the aforementioned sports? (See questions 7 and 8)

_____

12. Golf is a social sport. It allows for sociable conversation and cutting deals in a country club setting.

    Do you golf?   Yes _____   No _____

13. How inclined are you to take up the boss's favorite sports or hobby in order to get to know him or her better?

    Circle your choice.

    1   2   3   4   5   6   7   8   9   10
    Not   Very
    inclined   inclined

    Explain _____

14. Just a little fudging, a little white lie, a little cutting corners never hurt anything. Thus, it is OK for cheaters to be winners?

    Yes_____   No_____

    Explain_____

15. Is it cheating when a person embellishes their resume?

    1   2   3   4   5   6   7   8   9   10
    No   Yes

    Explain_____

Chapter 6

View the Conventional Wisdom Models with Healthy Skepticism

*There are not enough Indians in the world
to defeat the Seventh Calvary.*

George Armstrong Custer

It's Not Over Until I Win!

The oldest trick in the book - an ace up his sleeve.
Anyone worthy of being called an executive
knows how to get around the rules.

View the Conventional Wisdom Models with Healthy Skepticism

A truth told with bad intentions beats all the lies you can invent.
William Blake

People must think beyond the Conventional Wisdom Models and question the practices that comprise the existing social order of career advancement. The models falsely portray how the real world works. The Conventional Wisdom Models for Career Advancement presented in chapters 3, 4, and 5 were:

The Traditional Career Path Model
The Content of Character Model
The Sports Model

These models are problematical because they attempt to reduce complicated human behavior to very basic steps. They do not do justice to the role that politics plays in career advancement. For example, it seems very deceiving to tell people that all it takes to be a CEO is to have communication skills, integrity, passion, and vision. This conveys the message that career advancement is as simple as 1, 2, 3. From this perspective, the Conventional Wisdom Models represent reductionist thinking in its most damaging form. Given today's sophisticated workforce, some may perceive this level of thinking as an insult to their intelligence. On the face of it, the models appear altruistic and fill people with optimism, but they fail to explain how the promotion system actually functions. In many cases, this strong top-down control by management leads to a low tolerance for anyone who disagrees with their recipe for promotions.

Win Their Hearts and Minds

The genius of the Conventional Wisdom Models is that they convince people to place their careers in the hands of management.

View The Conventional Wisdom Models With Healthy Skepticism

Lying increases the creative faculties, expands the ego, and lessens the frictions of social contacts. Clare Boothe Luce

Does conventional career wisdom square with real world career reality? The answer is no. However, changing the penchant that some people have for the Conventional Wisdom Models is going to be difficult because we want to keep the democratic and rugged individualism values that they represent. Yet, the time has come to recognize how misleading they can be. These three vastly popular models present a classical approach-avoidance dilemma.

Are You Flameproof?

The beaming optimism of the Conventional Wisdom Models attracts people to them like moths to a flame. Avoid a flameout; be wary of the models' credibility gaps.

No matter how dubious the Conventional Wisdom Models are, they will not go away. They instill values and allow people to see the positive side of an organization. They create a promise of better things to come and a renewed confidence. These time honored models serve to initiate dialogue about a difficult and sometimes whimsical subject. They must be evaluated from the perspective of how they fit into the organization's culture and management's perspective of who gets promoted. Despite the fact that the Conventional Wisdom Models are flawed, they will continue to be perpetuated, even to the point of damaging relationships, because management and staff feel uncomfortable with publicly addressing career politics. It's not enough to have healthy skepticism; one needs tools (framework and questions) that work when analyzing the politics of promotion. As a career planning tool this book synthesizes a lot of information into a practical format. It echoes the fact that to be forewarned is to be forearmed.

The Conventional Wisdom Models
Are Here to Stay

That's not a lie, it's a terminological inexactitude. Winston Churchill

The Conventional Wisdom Models are ingrained in the psyche of the workplace for the following reasons:

- They take the edge off the frenzied realities that it takes to become a top executive.

- They provide a seemingly innocuous way to justify promotion decisions that have been made ahead of time.

- They reduce the complicated subject of career advancement to easily understood terms. This is done without ever having to mention complex concepts like promotion practices and politics.

- They keep hope of a promotion alive, but the need never seems to be fully satisfied. This may be cruel to people who are always runner-ups and believe that the organization is rooting for them.

- If management admits that the Conventional Wisdom Models are not fair, they will have to be revised to meet a new level of thinking.

- Many people are apprehensive of retaliation if they point out that the premise of the models and their practice are two different things.

If managers truly values employees, they must recognize the limitations of Conventional Wisdom Models and admit they have a strangle hold on career advancement. Then management and staff can explore how the Conventional Wisdom Models and the Real World Model can be used as a comparative framework for discussing the politics of promotion.

Demystifying the Conventional Wisdom Models
Does the Premise Match the Practice?

*A myth is a fixed way of looking at the world, which
cannot be destroyed, because looked at through the myth
all evidence supports the myth.*   Edward De Bono

Eventually the razzle dazzle fizzles out and you must deal with
reality. In order to see through the Conventional Wisdom Models
you must separate them from the ideals they claim to represent. As
shown below, this creates transparency into the false premise and
actual practice of executive behavior. The question then arises: to
what extent are the models practical or illusory?

Traditional Career Path Model	**Premise**	Keep the faith, baby! Work hard and you'll be discovered and promoted. Don't sully yourself with politics.
	Practice	Politics is the order of the day in advancement to the top. Ignoring politics increases vulnerabilities and decreases chances of advancement.
Content of Character Model	**Premise**	Only knights in shining armor need apply. Those with clean hands, pure of heart and mind become CEOs
	Practice	To succeed in a competitive world executives must be self-serving. However, they must conceal this in order to exploit opportunities and sway people to their view point.
Sports Model for Career Advancement	**Premise**	Winners always play by the rules.
	Practice	Winners sometimes do questionable things to win. In a way it's part of the culture of winning. The trick is to evade detection and not get caught because everyone loves a winner.

Is Conventional Wisdom
a Contradiction in Terms?

The enemy of conventional wisdom is not ideas but the march of events.
John Kenneth Galbraith

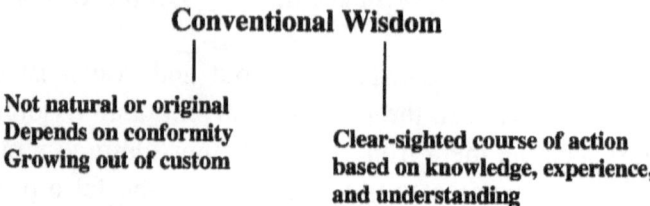

Conventional Wisdom

Not natural or original
Depends on conformity
Growing out of custom

Clear-sighted course of action
based on knowledge, experience,
and understanding

Webster's New World Dictionary

The term *conventional* refers to the organization's prescribed ways for moving up. Wisdom, on the other hand has to do with those things we esteem because they possess intrinsic value in and of themselves. Wisdom does not always lend itself to conventional thinking. However, to gain employee confidence the organization capitalizes on how the two represent the organization's ideals in practice and premise. In order to appreciate how the Conventional Wisdom Models are presented and sold to staff, students, and the public, review The Perfect Myth and the Content of Character Models. In a shot-gun wedding, the organization unites its prescription for advancement together with the popular idealized beliefs about advancement. For reasons of expediency, executives see them as being the same, and declare their merger a perfect marriage of values. This is done without checking to see if the models and ideals truly match the reality of the real world. Failure to do so causes staff to be disgruntled and disloyal.

Are You Running In Place?

Although some say that his or her values fit in with the Conventional Wisdom Models, the proof comes in the form of who gets promoted to the top and who gets passed over and for what reasons.

Conventional Wisdom:
A Contradiction in Terms?

For the great majority of mankind are satisfied with
appearances, as though they were realities, and are often more
influenced by the things that seem than those that are.
Niccolo Machiavelli

If it sounds too good to be true, it's probably not true. Results-oriented people use this rule to assess how a career model can limit or advance their careers. The Conventional Wisdom Models are controlled by executives who shape the playing field in order to control the promotion process. Because of the huge disparity in promotion power that exists between management and staff, it is easy for executives to hold up the Conventional Wisdom Model as the ideal. Many staff feel that it is this contradiction in power and control that makes the term Conventional Wisdom Model appear to be an oxymoron. Add to this the mad scramble for career advancement and it is easy to see how important distinctions can be overlooked. Jamming the two together without analysis leads people to confuse the models with the ideals, which are two separate things.

Little White Lies

An assessment of the Conventional Wisdom Models reflects that they have more to do with maintaining power and control in the workplace than with fairness.

The rub comes when people realize that their ideals are secondary to the goals of the models, which are to ensure conformity, as defined by the conventional organization. The second rub occurs when staff sense that although a person may demonstrate that he or she identifies with the organization's values, that identification does not guarantee anything. Hard work and competency merely guarantee a person the right to apply for higher positions and the right to hope.

Career Shaping Questions

1. **Lowering or raising the bar for advancement seems to have more to do with the managerial elite's perceptions and needs than with the true character of the individual selected for the position.**

    Circle your choice.

    Agree   1   2   3   4   5   6   7   8   9   10   Disagree

    Explain _____

2. **To what degree does the glass ceiling (artificial barriers that impede advancement such as bias against age, ethnicity, disability, gender, life style) exist in your organization?**

    Circle your choice.

    1   2   3   4   5   6   7   8   9   10

    There is no   Glass ceiling is
    glass ceiling.   firmly in place.

    Explain _____

Career Shaping Questions

3. **To what extent do you agree with the idea that hard work alone will get you to the top?**

   Circle your choice.

   Agree   1   2   3   4   5   6   7   8   9   10   Disagree

   Explain _____

4. **What personal and professional implications does career advancement politics have on an executive's ability to be a role model and lead people?**

   List personal implications for executives:

   _____

   List professional implications for executives:

   _____

5. **When a person is promoted to a management or executive position, do we get the best leader, the best politico, the best sycophant, or the best hybrid?**

   Select one of the following:

   Yes, the best leader   _____   Yes, the best politico_____

   Yes, the best sycophant_____   Yes, the best hybrid _____

   Explain_____

Chapter 7

The Surreal Model for Career Advancement

*Executives who claim that promotions are always based on
hard work and merit have mastered the ability to suspend reality.*
L. Flores

*Unless we talk about the politics of career advancement
we are contributing to our own oppression.*
L. Flores

Dance of the Cronies

The boss calls the tune and you dance to it.
And you said, you were an independent thinker,
your own man/woman. What happened?

You Might Be a Crony If:

1. You carpool with the boss - the designated driver
2. You're a political hack that covers the boss's back
3. You say "great idea, boss" after he or she speaks
4. You never seriously challenge the boss's decisions
5. You socialize mostly with the boss and his friends
6. You are privy to highly confidential insider information
7. You golf, tennis, workout, and drink with the boss
8. You think the term "crony" applies to the other guy
9. You join the same clubs and organizations as the boss
10. You and the boss share the same brain

The Surreal Model for Career Advancement

I believe in looking reality straight in the eye and denying it.
G. Keillor

Take it from the "kingmakers": no one makes it to a plush executive suite without a little help from someone behind the scenes. Exchanging favors, manipulating people, and exercising influence are the guiding principles of the Surreal Model.

Deep Denial

No one pursuing advancement to the top thinks of himself or herself as having received preferential treatment.

Studying promotion politics reveals that Private Preferential Treatment (PPT) is considered a professional requirement and private necessity. It's the lifeblood of a loosely connected shadow organization, which functions independently of any formal and objective criteria.

Who's Your Daddy?

Due to the seductiveness of comfort-zone politics, fairness has little to do with who gets promoted to the top.

Any soon-to-be executive knows that he or she needs the advantages and protective support of higher-ups. Only well-positioned managers can provide the opportunities that push people over the top. This makes PPT one of the organization's least discussed secrets. However, the Surreal Model cannot work unless certain things are in place. Namely, a super-structure that gives the people in charge anonymity, deniability, and distance between them and the unpopular decisions that are made in the name of doing what is best for the organization. This comes in the form of a mindset that fosters the development of the Laws of Private Preferential Treatment.

The Six Laws
of
Private Preferential Treatment

The good Lord set definite limits on man's wisdom,
but set no limits on his stupidity-and that's just not fair!
Konrad Adenauer

Behold the theater of the absurd. This section introduces the Laws of Private Preferential Treatment, which are the cornerstones of The Surreal Model. They represent the surprises that lurk below the surface and cause people to be shocked and awed unless they have some way to anticipate what is coming down the line. In the pages that follow, The Six Laws of Private Preferential Treatment are discussed in detail.

1. **Higher-ups override the organization's ideals of fair play and substitute their own promotion agenda.**

2. **Find a way to get pre-selected. Officially, the practice of preferential treatment is denied; unofficially, it is sanctioned.**

3. **Proteges receive priority in career advancement.**

4. **Externally advancement is driven by a hard work ethic.**

5. **Internally advancement turns on social similarities.**

6. **Advancement is reduced to a promotion machine maintained by staff and management.**

The aforementioned laws represent a juxtaposing of caustic ideas by a cabal of self-serving executives who want to secretly preserve the status quo–forever. Their creed is "keep your mouth shut and your mind closed."

Surreal Model For Career Advancement

There are no rules for career advancement. There are only traditions, customs, and hidden agendas.

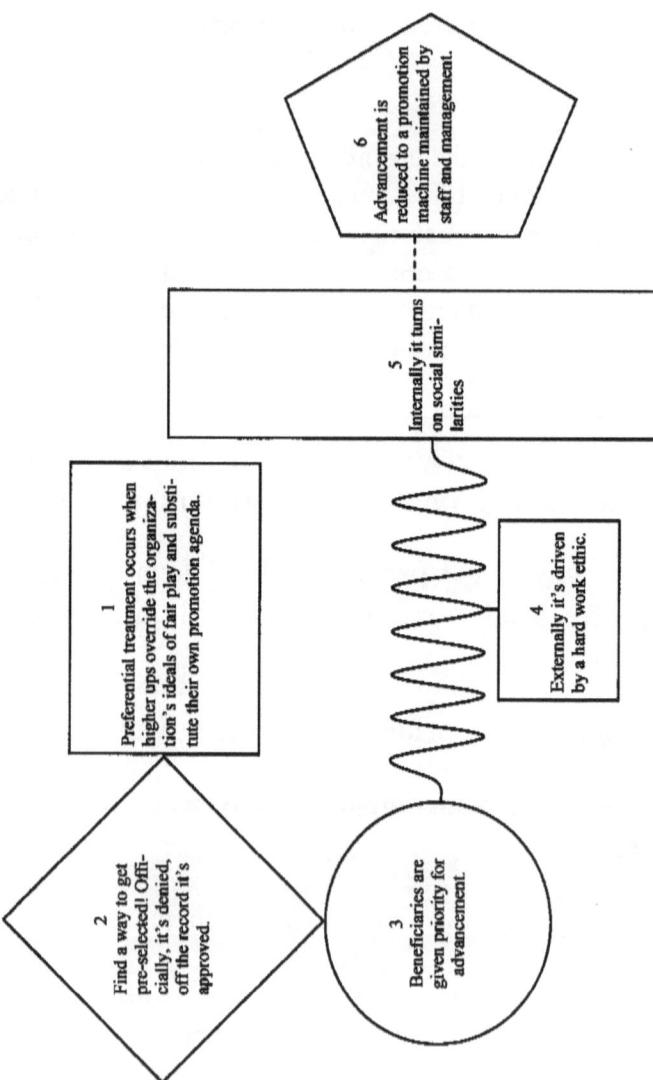

1
Preferential treatment occurs when higher ups override the organization's ideals of fair play and substitute their own promotion agenda.

2
Find a way to get pre-selected! Officially, it's denied, off the record it's approved.

3
Beneficiaries are given priority for advancement.

4
Externally it's driven by a hard work ethic.

5
Internally it turns on social similarities

6
Advancement is reduced to a promotion machine maintained by staff and management.

Law of Preferential Treatment
1.
Higher-ups override the organization's ideals of fair play and substitute their own promotion agendas.

Yesterday I was a dog. Today I am a dog.
Tomorrow I'll probably still be a dog. Snoopy

Keepers of the organization's secrets live by a code that requires them to safeguard the old career order. A flair for craftiness allows them to circumvent the organization's principles of "truth in action." This is the case whenever someone is the beneficiary of pre-selection for promotions.

The Sleaze Factor

Be smart enough to tell the truth but not dumb enough to tell the whole truth.

Anonymous

The politics of safeguarding the status quo is at the core of the Surreal Model for Career Advancement.

For legal purposes, decision makers announce that a position is open and go through the motions of interviewing applicants. A well-choreographed interview panel (or a semi-choreographed panel) creates the impression that things are on the up and up. In reality, the proceedings are a formality that conceals the fact that, ahead of time a "ringer" was chosen for the job. When this occurs, the interview process becomes utterly surreal. Hopeful job seekers sit before interview panels, "check out" the panelists' pasted-on smiles, and answer the scripted questions put forth. It makes one wonder how the interviewers can keep a straight face. As you enter the arena of career politics, don't take things personally. Find ways to keep from being discouraged by these types of charades.

Law of Preferential Treatment
1
Higher-ups override the organization's ideals of fair play and substitute their own promotion agendas.

The modern conservative is engaged in one of man's oldest exercises in moral philosophy; that is, the search for a superior moral justification for selfishness.   *John Kenneth Galbraith*

In some situations, if the desired person does not rank as one of the top three candidates, management rejects the list and repeats the process. This may occur until the pre-selected individual is within reach for hiring. In some instances the interview panel may be told who to promote and how to score the favored applicant. Surprisingly, decision makers do not view this as a surreal process. Nor is it flouting or nullifying the rules. It is simply interpreted as:

- Good business sense
- Hiring the best talent available
- Working in the best interest of the organization

Consequently, the ability to prevail by asserting executive prerogatives and influencing the promotion process is the trump card that decision makers can use to get their way.

When Executives Thumb Their Noses at Fairness
the Workplace Is Never the Same.

Pristine values are trampled when a favored person is moved to the head of the line, given a fast cut to the top, or provided with answers to the interview questions.

Law of Preferential Treatment
2.
Find a way to get pre-selected.
Officially, the practice is denied;
unofficially, it's given a wink and nod of approval.

*The fastest way to succeed is to look as if you're playing by other
people's rules, while quietly playing by your own.*
Michael Korda

Where there is no accountability, there is no fear of playing fast
and loose with the organization's promotion practices. Knowing
how to play dumb and exploit ambiguous situations has its place in
executive decision making. Once a person has received the cue to
advance he or she must walk in lock-step with the boss.

That's Just the Way Things Are Done Here

**When no one takes responsibility for the informal
promotion practices, the process takes on a life of its own.**

Since nobody is held to answer, this free-wheeling process allows
people to justify their promotion by presenting what appear to be
socially acceptable explanations. This stretching of the truth occurs
even when the deciding officials and the pre-selected individual
know that the real facts, motives, and actions are different.

Your Nose Is Growing

**The perfect pre-selection process
requires room for plausible denial.**

Law of Preferential Treatment
2
Find a way to get pre-selected.
Officially, the practice is denied;
unofficially, it's given a wink and nod of approval.

The very clever know how to hide their cleverness.
Francois de La Rochefoucauld

In the event of unforseen complications, managers must have the maximum possible room for claiming that they were unaware of the pre-selection activities. "I was out of the loop" is the statement made by people who want to exonerate themselves from activities they participated in. They do not want their name associated with cheating. As a result of management's tendencies towards pre-selection, an organization may develop a profoundly split personality. The word bipolar condition is an apt description.

The Art of Preferential Treatment

Act as if you know
that they know
that you know
that to receive it you must
behave as if you don't
know you're getting it!
Lorenzo Flores

This could be termed "management by escape hatch," since it enables some executives to have it both ways. Executives are quick to claim that private preferential treatment does not exist. However, many find or invent ways that allow them to continue providing privileges to people that they favor. This leads to the perception that cronyism trumps competency.

Law of Preferential Treatment
3.
Beneficiaries are systematically groomed and given priority for advancement.

What men call friendship is often just an arrangement for mutual gain.
Francois de La Rochefoucauld

Acting expeditiously and without accountability is the aim of this outrageously Surreal Model. Power, in this sense, means being able to shift the blame and not be held fully accountable for one's actions. Working away from public view, higher-ups can decide who in their "mind's eye" is the most desirable for advancement.

Career Reality Check

Unrestrained by formal rules,
management and staff can lower or raise the bar for
promotions as they see fit.

We are often more liked for our defects
than for our qualities.
Francois de La Rochefoucauld

Because it's done surreptitiously, the process of channeling people into certain positions is a clandestine quota system. It is an elite quota system because the highest paying and most powerful executive positions are set aside for certain types of people. Historically, white males have been made to feel by the organization that they are the only ones who can protect the status quo of career advancement and carry the torch of progress forward. This seemingly well veiled selection process is carried out under the guise of "matching the right person for the right job" or selecting the proverbial "well-rounded person."

Law of Preferential Treatment
4.
Advancement to the top is reduced to a promotion machine, maintained by managers and staff

Politics, n. A strife of interest masquerading as a contest of principles.
Ambrose Bierce

As if using a system of levers and pulleys, executives are highly skilled at positioning people for advancement. In some organizations, when vacancies occur a good number of "choice positions" are not advertised or are kept very low profile. By doing so management can move in someone it prefers for the top jobs. In many cases the promotion process has all the markings and movements of a political cloning machine. It promotes people on the basis of how useful they are personally and professionally to the organization's agenda. It seems that almost automatically, many of the top positions are set aside for a few chosen people.

Send in the Clones

All of the working parts on the pre-selection assembly line must be well oiled and coordinated, e.g., mentoring, opportunities, and exposure to the right people.

In order to shape and mold the person to fit the organization culture and climate, the promotion mechanism must function as a finely tuned and well-lubricated unit. The end product of this surreal power-driven system is a top-of-the-line executive who meets the organization's ideal blueprint specifications. It appears that what were once fundamental hard work ethics free of politics have been replaced by politically-oriented hard work ethics. For all the talk about ethical rules for career advancement none are ever posted for viewing. All that exist are traditions and customs which management puts to their own use.

Law of Preferential Treatment
5.

On the surface, career advancement is driven by hard work

The trick in politics is to sustain the illusions of progress and change while preserving the freeze-frame of the status quo.
Lewis H. Lapham

No one makes it to the top without having a strong work ethic and engaging in workplace politics. Which one of these is more important depends on the lead set by management. Organizations have survival instincts which tell them that promotions must always project the idea that they have been properly grounded in common sense. For purposes of saving face, on the surface at least, there must be the appearance of always meeting the unbending promotion standards of:

Hard Work and Competency
Going above and beyond the call of duty-showing tireless energy. Zero tolerance for mistakes. Knowing the job backwards and forwards.

Loyalties
Working within the guidelines and policies. Indulging your superiors. Make the boss look good.

Integrity
Insisting that the organization's promotion practices are above reproach. As honest as the day is long.

For all practical purposes, this is a well-orchestrated public relations effort. Supporters of the Surreal Model try to put a positive spin on it, even when they know they are deluding themselves and playing mind games with people.

Law of Preferential Treatment
6.

After all is said and done, advancement turns on hardwork, social similarities, and connections

The superior man understands what is right:
the inferior man understands what will sell. Confucius

How do some people climb so fast and high on the career ladder? This has to do with hard work, social similarities, appearances, and connections. Also, there is an invisible executive hand at work selecting the (so called) right person for the right job. Executives, feeling that they must be careful about deciding who gets promoted, control the major facets of the evaluation and succession planning process for key positions. Besides the formal ways of evaluating people, the organization sizes up workers on the basis of personality and social climbing style.

Market Thyself

To move up the career ladder, one must become proficient in extracurricular activities, such as dining, hunting, fishing, golfing, and shooting the bull (BS-ing). These must be done well for you to be welcomed into the elite, insiders group.

Organizations are interested on return on investment (ROI). Because executives are viewed as investments, their spouses may be interviewed to see if they meet management's expectations. Clearly, to be a CEO you must marry someone who wants you to be a CEO. You and your spouse are a team and it takes team effort to get ahead. Your spouse must match your drive for advancement and do whatever is necessary to help you. Sometimes marrying the boss's son or daughter or a person of notoriety can be a good career move. Besides romance a marriage incorporates a business partnership for financial gain. In a materialistic, status seeking, and image prone society this money making side of marriage is part of the promotion machine process.

Law of Preferential Treatment
6
After all is said and done, advancement turns on hard work, social similarities, and connections

The best way for a young man who is without friends or influence to begin is:

> *First, to get a position,*
> *Second to keep his mouth shut;*
> *Third, observe;*
> *Fourth, be faithful;*
> *Fifth, make his employer think he*
> *would be lost in a fog without him:*
> *Sixth, be polite.   Russell Sage*

Go to an upscale restaurant and order an appetizer of escargot and hear the waiter say, "Fine selection, Sir/Madam." A person who wants to move up must demonstrate that he or she is a connoisseur of food and drink. Making the rounds of the cocktail circuit and feasting on fine cuisine should never come into play. However, get-togethers are often used to size up people and find out information-up close and personal. Baiting people into revealing themselves is easily done after they have consumed alcohol–some become chatter boxes. From a career advancement perspective, these activities are not seen as pretentious; instead they are rationalized as personal investments that may reap career dividends for the boss and the person being studied and measured. Know your strong suit. Know your boss's strong suit. Know your rivals strong suit. By asking seemingly harmless questions and making innocent sounding comments people intend to size you up by finding out things like:

Who are your heros or heroines?
What experiences have shaped your life?
When are you at your best?
What emotion do you find hard to control?
Where do you want to go in life?
Why do you think and act the way you do?
Will you be an average or outstanding co-worker or CEO?
How do you overcome adversity? How do you define success?

This form of gathering information is a two-way street. The questions above should be used (without alcohol) by all concerned to determine their level of comfort and commitment to the organization. In other words, if you don't play the game, you can't win. You must be in it to win.

Fear of Fairness a Surreal Phobia

We reward small virtues and big vices.   Paul Eldridge

Paranoia in career advancement is real because there are people who will misrepresent the facts and undermind your work. When the organization bottom line is about dollars and the competition for promotions is heavy, it is easy to become numb to the idea of fairness. The organizational acculturation process inculcates people with a particular way of thinking and acting in accordance with the organization's expectations of a wannabe executive. Part of career advancement is volunteering to be desensitized from the warm ideals of faith in one's fellow man to the harsh realities that we constantly bump up against people who are merciless in getting their way.

An Organization Is Only As Sick As Its Secrets

The desensitization process does not eliminate values, it permeates values so that a person becomes more malleable to the organization's needs.

The people most susceptible to desensitization of their feelings are those who hunger with ambition and never question the organization's practices. Desensitization transforms an individual from a caring person to one that uses people as pawns in a game of chess. The list below identifies the cluster of warning signs manifested by people who aspire to advance in a surreal organization.

Dynamics of Desensitization

- Lacks empathy for people
- Unfair profiteering, keeping double books
- Manipulating everything to one's advantage
- Proficiency at saying one thing and doing another
- Treacherous diplomatic trickery and double dealing
- Opportunistic exploitation via politically driven agendas
- Insulating the boss from blame by blaming other people
- Cover up. Never reveals sources and methods of operation
- Uses character assassination—rumors, innuendoes, slander

Summary

We must select the illusion which appeals to our temperament and embrace it with passion, if we want to be happy. Cyril Connolly

Being mesmerized by the possibilities of a promotion and tired of continually competing for advancement causes some people to resort to politicking. For people who believe in fairness the Surreal Model represents an assault on all of their sensibilities.

Dazed and Confused
The dense fog of Promotion Politics can move in so quickly that a person can lose sight of his or her principles.

Ethics in career advancement politics are always questioned.

1. Careerist are always ethical   Yes _____ No _____

2. Careerist have flexible ethics   Yes _____ No _____

For surreal reasons, some people may assume that they have inferential relationships with superiors. They tend to overstate their relationships with the "big cheese" and head honchos. This may be true for people who car pool with the boss or participate in activities with him or her. What may follow are a lot of unintended consequences in which imaginative conjecturing leads people to believe that they have special relationships with higher ups. Ambitious careerist may overrate themselves by feeling that preferential treatment is automatically bestowed through devotion to duty and connections. In the minds of careerist, this emboldens them and generates perceptions that they are worthy of special considerations for opportunities and rewards.

Do You Have a Moral Compass?
The degree to which Private Preferential Treatment occurs hinges on how leaders manage their personal and professional relationships with staff.

Summary

Your mind must always go, even while you're shaking hands and going through all the maneuvers. I developed the ability long ago to do one thing while thinking another. Richard M. Nixon

This also, has a lot to do with how management talks about and models Career Advancement Ethics from the top down. To what extent does management embrace the concept of Career Advancement Ethics? Or is it shrugged aside with a big yawn? Some people are perplexed by the natural love-hate relationship that exists towards career advancement politics. At some level they need it, but at another level they reject it as if it were a sinful act. It is this complex interplay of human and organizational dynamics that drives preferential treatment underground, where it becomes a matter of privacy and necessity for the parties involved. Because of this secrecy, the way in which it plays itself out makes it seem repulsive unless one believes in the use of preferential treatment as a means to help others, improve the organization, and position oneself for advancement. In reality, the politics of preferential treatment as it relates to advancement is a concept that some say does not exist, yet it continues to appear in various forms. As a fact of life it impacts all phases of career development. Unfortunately, in the end, this intense career focus may cause a self-centered, myopic view of what it takes to move up the ranks.

Without Clear Political Boundaries People Tend to Get Ahead at the Expense of Others

Without official rules for career advancement, the mixture of hard work, being extended privileges by the boss, and reciprocity opens the door to creatively justifying an assortment of perceived entitlements.

Summary

We look for it and do not see it; Its name is The Invisible.
We listen to it and do not hear it; Its name is The Inaudible.
We touch it and do not find it; Its name is the Formless
                    Lao-tzu (604 531 B.C.)

The Surreal Model does not blur things together; it literally erases all of the ethical boundaries for promotions. This is why it is so easy for staff to become desensitized to the idea of fairness in the workplace. For example, it's said that private, preferential treatment does not exist. Yet, some believe they have earned a right to it. How can one earn a right to something that is nonexistent? No problem! In career politics the definition of perks and "bennies" can be stretched as far as management permits. The idea of being entitled to special privileges is not far fetched when executives are overtly, or covertly, aiding people they prefer to promote. Having an in with the boss provides a sense of security.

The Joker Is Wild

The Surreal Organization does not steal your soul;
it just nibbles away at the edges.

Lorenzo Flores

The web of private, preferential treatment grows by leaps and bounds if management condones a "You scratch my back and I'll scratch your back" philosophy. Without management setting a proper example, an entitlement mentality can permeate the entire organizational hierarchy.

We have met the enemy and he is us.

Walt Kelly

When a deep analysis of the organization's promotion practices is done, no executive can escape the reality, the use, and the impact of career advancement politics on his or her upward mobility.

Career Shaping Questions

1. **Within the context of the Surreal Model, how do people become desensitized to values and ethics? What motivates them to do whatever it takes to get promoted?**

   Explain _____

2. **Is it possible to reverse the desensitization process so that people will look out for each other's best interest?**

   Mark your choice:

   Yes_____   No_____

   Explain your reasoning:

   _____

3. **At work what things seem to feed your boss's ego?**

   Explain_____

4. **At work what things seem to feed your ego?**

   Explain_____

Career Shaping Questions

5. **Besides being a hard worker, a person must receive preferential treatment (uncommon support from higher-ups) in order to make it to the top.**

   Circle your choice.

   Never 1   2   3   4   5   6   7   8   9   10   Always

   Explain _____

6. **At mid-management and above, what percentage of the positions do you feel are filled by pre-selection - someone handpicked for the position ahead of time.**

   Circle your choice.

   10%   20   30   40   50   60   70   80   90   100%

   Explain _____

7. **To be or not to be**
   To fit the organization's mold or not to fit it - 'Tis the Question'

   Select A or B below.

   A. The job makes the person _____

   B. The person makes the job _____

   Explain _____

There is a direct correlation between how far a person rises up the career ladder and the amount of peer pressure he or she feels to uphold the organization's formal and informal expectations. The goal is to be a company man or woman who fits the executive mold as defined by the managerial elite.

Career Shaping Questions

8. **Depending on management's definition of "fitting in," a person can be set up for success, for failure, or marginalized.**

   Circle your choice.

   Never   1   2   3   4   5   6   7   8   9   10   Always

   Explain _____

9. **To what degree does career advancement politics cause morale problems in the workplace?**

   Circle your choice.

   Never   1   2   3   4   5   6   7   8   9   10   Always

   Explain _____

10 **To what degree does career advancement politics cause productivity problems in the workplace?**

   Circle your choice.

   Never   1   2   3   4   5   6   7   8   9   10   Always

   Explain _____

Career Shaping Questions

11. To what degree does your organization's culture (the way we do things here) perpetuate Promotion Politics?

Circle your choice.

1   2   3   4   5   6   7   8   9   10
No   Extremely
politics   political

Explain _____

12. To what degree can the promotion process (interviews, test, selection panel) be influenced if the organization wants to promote a particular person?

Circle your choice.

1   2   3   4   5   6   7   8   9   10
Never   Always
happens   happens

Explain _____

13. Talent will get you only so far. What else belongs in a person's repertoire of professional and personal skills?

Explain _____

Career Shaping Questions

14. **What informal things have you done or have you seen co-workers do in order to get in good with the boss, e.g., bring newspaper clippings, ski trips, cook boss's favorite food?**

    List things co-workers have done.

    _____   _____

    _____   _____

    List things you have done.

    _____   _____

    _____   _____

15. **Once a person has reached the executive level, what informal skills (off the record things) does it take to maintain his or her position? List specific things.**

    _____

16. **List the things that you control in your career advancement?**

    _____   _____

    _____   _____

Career Shaping Questions

17. If a person "politics" his or her way to the top by using, hard work, self-serving behavior, dedication, charm, and influence, what implications does being a "politico" have on his or her ability to inspire trust and, confidence, and lead by example?

Circle your choice.

1	2	3	4	5	6	7	8	9	10

I trust   I do not trust
this person   this person

Explain_____

18. Cronyism occurs when the boss's close friends receive favoritism. Does cronyism trump competency? When the boss hires friends without regard for their qualifications, does this convey that friendships supersede competency? Or is the boss doing as he or she says: hiring the best person available?

Circle your choice.

1	2	3	4	5	6	7	8	9	10

No, cronyism   Yes, cronyism
never trumps   always trumps
competency   competency

Explain_____

Career Shaping Questions

19. **Gaining exposure to the right people. In your organization, what social and recreational activities seem linked to upward mobility? How much of a role do you take in planning and organizing them?**

Social activities may range from special events to the dinner-cocktail circuit. Recreational activities may range from parlor games to yachting.

List social activities	Check those you actively participate in	List recreational activities	Check those you actively participate in
_____	_____	_____	_____
_____	_____	_____	_____
_____	_____	_____	_____

Total up the number of social and recreational activities you participate in _____

Chapter 8

Fairness: A Revolutionary Concept
in
Career Advancement Politics

More than anything else,
followers want to believe that their leaders are ethical and honest.
They want to say, "Someday I want to be like him or her."
Secrets of Effective Leadership

Executive 101:
Survival Skills

Learn how to ask tough hardball questions
and accept lame answers.

Fairness: A Revolutionary Concept in Career Advancement Politics

A good executive is one who makes people contentedly settle for less than they meant to get, and in return for more than they meant to give. *M. McLaughlin*

'Fairness-Bring it on!' Ideally, fairness is about people putting aside personal feelings and looking out for one another's welfare. For fairness to become a reality, people must replace their biases with objective thoughts. This is a difficult but important task.

Is the Glass Half Full, Half Empty, or Leaking?

The degree of commitment received by the boss is inversely related to the degree of fairness subordinates feel they receive from him or her.

Fairness in Career Advancement is a state of mind and action. It is a mental process driven by a desire to make objective decisions when it comes to promotions. At the action level, it requires acts of performance, which reflect the qualities of being just and unbiased. Pristine fairness, like pure democracy, is a goal worth the struggle. However, it seems that fairness in promotions is something that most executives have a difficult time putting into practice. Higher-ups are not always rational actors. They sometimes bypass logic and reason when it comes to promoting people in their comfort zone.

Our Fearless Leader

Absolute fairness in promotion practices is a radical thought. We don't want to make changes ahead of their time. We must proceed slowly with this new idea.

In the end, fairness tends to be diluted by egotistical behavior, which reduces executives to an attitude of "me firstism" when it comes to dealing with people.

Fair Play in Career Advancement

Ethics stays in the prefaces of the average business science book.
Peter Drucker

Having 100% functional fair employment practices represents the pinnacle of organizational fairness. *Fair employment practices* refers to treating people equally, in accordance with the law. It means being objective enough to promote a person strictly on merit and independent of factors such as appearance, religion, age, height, weight, race, and disability.

Is Perception Reality?

In the mind of executives, fairness means giving up power and control over people, resources, and promotions. They feel this could diminish their status in the eyes of other executives.

The following list highlights important areas of professional development in which fairness plays a crucial career-shaping role. For a level playing field to exist, fairness must be present in the following areas:

Assignments	**Reward System**
Employee Evaluations	**Promotion Practices**
Information Sharing	**Opportunities**
Rights	**Privileges**
Competition	**Resource Allocation**
Mentoring	**Recognition-give due credit**

What makes fairness hard to come by is the fact that it is difficult to be objective when it comes to one's personal self-interest. Everyone has difficulty setting aside feelings, which influence his or her decisions. Without reality checks and a commitment to Career Advancement Ethics, the Surreal Model for Career Advancement will take root and overpower the other career advancement models presented in this text.

Career Shaping Questions

1. **When it comes to promotions, how does your boss define playing fair?**

   _____

   _____

2. **When it comes to promotions, how do you define playing fair?**

   _____

   _____

3. **If you were the boss would you give up the power to promote, e.g., the final say on who gets promoted and who does not get promoted?**

   1   2   3   4   5   6   7   8   9   10
   Yes, give up   Never give up
   promotion power   promotion power

   Explain_____

Career Shaping Questions

4. **Executive Empathy in Career Advancement Politics: Do executives tend to the career needs of subordinates with the same intensity that they nurture their own careers?**

   Circle your choice.

   1   2   3   4   5   6   7   8   9   10

   Boss pays no   **Boss gives my**
   attention to my   **career the same**
   career needs   **attention s/he gives**
                                his or her own career

   Explain _____

5. **Executive Moral Values in Career Advancement Politics: The actions taken by higher-ups in promoting people to key positions always reflect high ethical standards?**

   Circle your choice.

   1   2   3   4   5   6   7   8   9   10

   No Ethics   **100% Ethical**

   Explain _____

Career Shaping Questions

6. **If you could ask your boss two questions about the Politics of Promotion, what would they be?**

   A. _____

   B. _____

7. **If you were to ask your peer rivals, (co-workers) two questions about promotion politics, what would they be?**

   A. _____

   B. _____

8. **The numbers tell it all. During the past five to ten years how many formal and informal complaints has the organization had regarding its promotion practices?**

   Informal number _____ Formal number_____

9. **How many of these formal complaints have been sustained in favor of the organization? Number _____**

10. **How many of these formal complaints have been sustained in favor of the complainant? Number _____**

11. **How were the informal complaints handled?**
    Explain_____

Chapter 9

A New Paradigm
for
Career Advancement

*It is difficult to get a man to understand something
when his salary depends upon his not understanding it.*
Upton Sinclair

Sheer Political Genius

You have Aladdin's magic lamp and the power to change your career. Everyone has an inner political genie. Once you let the political genie out, you can began to transform your career.

A New Paradigm
for
Career Advancement

Men stumble over the truth from time to time,
but
most pick themselves up and hurry off as if nothing happened.
Winston Churchill

It is in the best interest of your career to be fluent in career speak because it is a window to the soul of the organization. Speaking the language of career advancement can decrease your chances of becoming a victim of promotion politics. This entails changing the paradigm that many people have about politics. Typically, a paradigm is the way that a person puts together his or her perception of the world. The paradigm that many people have been taught regarding the politics of promotion is that politicking for advancement is bad. It's something that no decent human being would ever do. Generally, people are encouraged to frown upon the words "workplace politics." This is done without ever questioning why they are supposed to show displeasure with the term, when in reality political leverage is one of the main ingredients needed for advancement. When it comes to career advancement politics we need a new paradigm, which reflects integrity, individuality, and the actualities of the workplace.

People Can Handle Change; It's the
Transition That's Difficult.

New Career Advancement Paradigm Relies On:
Hard work and pro-active career thinking to get ahead.

vs.

Old Career Advancement Paradigm
Rely on hard work to get ahead.

Manage Your Career Expectations

- Promotions are 80% hard work and 20% politics
- How did you get your job? Answer: "I knew somebody."
- Know your blind spots and your rival's Achilles heel

Contrasting
the
Career Advancement Paradigms

The degree of one's emotions varies inversely
with one's knowledge of the facts.
Bertrand Russell

Old Paradigm	**New Paradigm**
Rely on hard work to get ahead	**Rely on hard work and pro-active career thinking to get ahead**
Hard work is its own reward	Hard work and pro-active politics are part of career advancement
You make it on your own	Develop power base of people and resources
Never seek favors	Practice responsible reciprocity Do good by helping others
Never question the boss about promotion practices	Understand the boss and work with his or her limitations. Learn to read tendencies.
Don't be a sellout. Negative term used by persons unsure of how to market their skills	Grasp the difference between selling out your morals and selling (marketing) your skills

Contrasting
the
Career Advancement Paradigms

"It has always seemed strange to me," said Doc.
"The things we admire in men, kindness, generosity,
openness, honesty, understanding and feeling are
the concomitants of failure in our system. And those
traits we detest, sharpness, greed, acquisitiveness, and
egotism and self-interest are the traits of success. And
while men admire the qualities of the first they love the
produce of the second."   *John Steinbeck*

The old paradigm is locked into the status quo, which defines career advancement in such a narrow way that it leaves little room for other beliefs or opinions. It is tantamount to viewing career advancement with blinders, which limits one's career development. By changing paradigms a person is in a better position to get the most out of his or her best talents and potential.

The new Career Advancement Paradigm looks at what can happen when an individual harnesses his or her full social, political, and economic potential.

The Best Career Advancement Tools Are:
· **The Ability to Re-Create Yourself**
· **The Ability to Re-define Circumstances Around You**

This book encourages people to reevaluate their beliefs and relationships concerning career advancement and the politics of promotion. This includes developing the ability to link up with people and appreciate (1) the art of reciprocity, (2) interdependencies, and (3) alliances that augment one's goals.

The pendulum swung furiously to the left,
because it had been drawn too far to the right. Lord Macaulay

The Art of Reciprocity

Reciprocity refers to how people position themselves so that they can be of assistance to others. This opens the door to building relationships and information gathering.

Understanding Interdependencies

This points to the who, what, when, where, why, and how relationships are nurtured and maintained by staff and management in the organization.

Building Alliances

This pertains to how a person develops selective networks of people, both inside and outside the organization. It stands to reason that the more networking connections that a person has, the more protection and resources he or she possesses in time of need.

When the above traits are placed into action, a paradigm shift begins to occur. It moves a person to revise his or her learned patterns of behavior and see that politics, when used in a healthy way, can be a positive force for change. Career maintenance requires a person to continually redefine career politics in a way that he or she can live with. Politics can be proactive when a person is able to anticipate things and gather the resources to deal with the situation. One does this by engaging in critical thinking, which can bring about constructive changes to one's career and the workplace.

Question Authority Or Get Fooled

Nothing is going to change in the arena of promotion politics unless people are ready, willing, and able to discuss the politics of promotion in a frank manner.

This book provides a framework for discussing career development, career maintenance, and career politics.

Unless You Talk About It, The Joke Is On You

Summary

The last of the human freedoms
to choose one's attitude
in any given
set of circumstances,
to choose one's own way.
                    Viktor Frankl

Many people have trouble acknowledging that promotion politics exists, let alone embracing the idea that it has a language of its own. To do so might cancel out a lot of what he or she has said about promotions being fair. Thus, making sense out of the role that politics plays in the promotion process has always been a daunting task. It's not that people don't talk about it; they discuss it around the water cooler or in the parking lot. Without the benefit of a framework for analysis the conversations tend to be filled with hearsay, emotions, and superficiality.

A Question for the Ages

The question is not whether Career Advancement Politics is discussed, but what is the quality and quantity of the dialogue?

Do the discussions lead to profound changes in the organization's promotion practices or superficial tinkering?

The reality is that the organization's political propaganda machine, promotion practices, and office rumor mill are not going to disappear. Therefore, everyone must find his or her own constructive ways to cope with these issues. This requires people to make personal decisions about their lives and how they will manage their careers. This is why people must challenge their personal assumptions and management's promotion practices. Probing and questioning will lead to positive changes and new paradigms in the way that people view competition and career advancement in the workplace.

Career Shaping Questions

1. **If you could change the boss's perspective on promotion practices, what would it be?**

   _____

2. **If the boss could change your perspective on promotion practices, what would it be?**

   _____

3. **Given your organization's promotion practices, what new professional and personal skills do you need to develop in order to move up the career ladder?**

   Professional Skills _____

   Personal Skills _____

4. **Sometimes bosses tell staff "There are no limits to how far you can go in this organization." How well does this match with the hard realities of career advancement politics?**

   True   1   2   3   4   5   6   7   8   9   10   False

   Explain _____

5. **Best career advancement advice you have received?**

   _____

6. **Worse career advancement advice you have received?**

   _____

Chapter 10

Do Organizations Have the Political Will to Talk About the Politics of Promotion?

Men fear thought as they fear nothing else on earth-more than ruin-more than even death...

Thought is subversive and revolutionary, destructive and terrible, thought is merciless to privilege, established institutions and comfortable habit.

Thought looks into the pit of hell and is not afraid.

Thought is great and swift and free, the light of the world and the chief glory of man.

Bertrand Russell

Denying Reality

It takes big balls to talk about the politics of promotion.
Many executives prefer discussing the old standbys:
leadership, communication, teamwork, management
skills, and customer service. Thus, many staff members
view the boss as being an "out of touch elitist" when it comes to
discussing the realities of career advancement.

Reality Bites

The more that higher-ups insist that all promotions are strictly
based on merit and hard work the more questions need to
be asked about the organization's promotion practices.

Do Organizations Have the Political Will to Talk About the Politics of Promotion?

Something unpleasant is coming when men
are anxious to tell the truth. Benjamin Disraeli

A person may have the political clout to beat rivals, but may not have the political will to talk about what they did to get to the top. You can tell a lot about a person from the way that he or she got promoted. For some people, one of the hardest things to discuss is the role that politics has played in their careers. The following framework provides an overview of how this subject might be approached. The language of career advancement incorporates the three career advancement models presented in this text:

The Real World Model
Perspectives on career advancement in today's highly competitive workplace. Surviving in a pressure cooker of paradoxes is the order of the day.

The Conventional Wisdom Models
Describe how things work in an ideal world marked by truth, honor, and merit.

The Surreal Model
Details how things work when no one is held accountable for the organization's promotion practices.

People who are interested in upward mobility understand these models and use them as points of reference when discussing career advancement.

Speak the Language of Reality

The action framework presented in this book can be an effective way to initiate and maintain a dialogue about career advancement politics.

A great many people think they are thinking when they
are merely rearranging their prejudices. William James

Sometimes a person may not be fully aware of the issues that make up his or her point of view and how he or she is coming across to a person who has a different opinion. The diagram on page 226 pulls together the three career advancement models (Conventional Wisdom, Real World, and Surreal) and provides an overview of the way in which people discuss career politics.

**What Is Your
Career Game Plan?**

**In Promotion Politics a person must be able to
analyze the mental frame of reference that he or she
is speaking from and know the pros and cons of each
model.**

All three models may coexist in an organization. Frequent reality checks serve to keep the models separate in one's mind, ensure positive decisions, and maintain a healthy work environment. A person knowledgeable about promotion politics knows the strengths and weaknesses of the models. When discussing them he or she will tactfully move to achieve a balanced approach by bringing the conversation around to the Real World Model. By doing this, reference can be made to the various career advancement concepts and how they apply to a person's career planning. In the following diagram (based on Eric Berne's concept of Transactional Analysis) **A** and **B** are discussing career advancement from two different perspectives (dotted line). **A** is discussing it from the Conventional Wisdom view point while **B** is discussing it from the Surreal approach. The solid line reflects the best way to discuss promotion politics which is to have a firm grasp of the realities of what it takes to be promoted. By integrating the career advancement models into his or her way of thinking, a person is able to discuss promotion politics in a way that demonstrates that he or she can analyze issues rationally and pose constructive alternatives.

Communicating Across the Models: The Language of Career Advancement Politics

Beliefs

Boss has your best interest in mind.

Work hard and you will be discovered and promoted. The promotion process is fair.

The X Factor

A person's rate of career advancement depends on performance, potential, and likeability as defined by others.

Reality is whatever you can get away with.

Bosses promote people in their comfort zone—who follow orders a.k.a. lacky, crony, hatchet man.

A

| Conventional Wisdom Model |
| Real World Model |
| Surreal World Model |

B

| Conventional Wisdom Model |
| Real World Model |
| Surreal World Model |

Beliefs

Performance is all that counts.

You are 100% in charge of your career. It's all up to you.

Career advancement is made up of hard work, appearances, and connections. You control 80% and management controls 20% of your career.

Find a way to get pre-selected. Everything is rigged.

It's a dog-eat-dog world. You have to do it to them before they do it to you.

Discussing Career Advancement Politics

Truth is always subversive. Anne Lamott

The main advantages in talking about promotion politics are that it prevents problems, creates transparency, and increases the level of trust between upper management and staff. Depending on how one sees it, the major disadvantage in talking about the politics of promotion is that it reveals the truth. There are no miracle words or silver bullets, and no one-size-fits-all approach to career advancement. The only thing that seems to make a difference is honest dialogue. In order to foster discussion in a sensible way, rather than a trial and error process, the author suggests exploring issues by using a blend of Socratic Questioning and Critical Thinking Skills.

A. Socratic Questioning This involves the skill of systematically asking reflective questions. It is a logical approach to challenging one's assumptions and weighing the consequences of one's actions. It may be used to seek answers from a group view point or from an organizational perspective.

B. Critical Thinking The focus is on finding the truth, eliminating bias, and considering one's options. A thought provoking personal inventory helps a person to better evaluate, analyze, and interpret his or her career decisions.

The Truth About Career Advancement Politics Will Make You Stronger And Wiser

---

Apply critical thinking to executive decisions. What is the interplay of the following factors in the promotion process?

- Discretion   Power to judge or act on one's will or fancy
- Discrimination   Bias treatment based on class vs. individual merit
- Ethics   Code of moral values to live by - honesty, integrity
- Favoritism   Act of being unfairly partial. Your bias is showing
- Prerogative   Exclusive right or privilege to do as one pleases

Discussing Career Advancement Politics

*Men in authority will always think that criticism
of their policies is dangerous. They will always equate
their policies with patriotism, and find criticism subversive.*
Henry Steele Commager

The aforementioned social action framework (Communicating Across the Models, page 226) reflects how complicated the thinking process can become when a person is trying to answer the question "How do I get promoted?" Talking about career advancement from the standpoint of a social action framework has the benefit of helping people change their career advancement paradigm. The advantages of this analytical framework are:

1. It speaks to the fact that questions are the answers when it comes to unraveling the politics of promotions. Precise questions unmask the pretentiousness and mystery that sometimes surrounds fuzzy career advancement practices.

2. It enables a person to compare and contrast career advancement models. This empowers people to see career advancement from a holistic big picture point of view.

3. It allows someone to systematically isolate issues for discussion.

4. It enables a person to integrate the language of career advancement into his or her vocabulary, as well as into everyday job survival skills.

5. It emphasizes that there is a professional, personal, and business side to career advancement.

6. It enables a person to learn from different career advancement styles.

7. It helps you decide how you will survive and thrive in the arena of workplace politics.

Career Shaping Questions

1. List the "hot button" issues (words that trigger emotional feelings) that arise when the subject of Politics of Promotion is discussed.

   _____   _____   _____

   _____   _____   _____

2. A common practice among co-workers is to help each other out. When you help someone, do you expect him or her to return the favor?

   Circle your choice.

   Never   1   2   3   4   5   6   7   8   9   10   **Always**

   Explain _____

3. You can tell a lot about a person's ethics and values from the way that he or she got promoted to the top.

   Circle your choice.

1	2	3	4	5	6	7	8	9	10
Agree								**Disagree**	
with								**with**	
statement								**statement**	

   Explain_____

Career Shaping Questions

4. **Anyone who wants to become an executive must be proficient in certain skills. In the race to the top of the executive career ladder, which comes first: Leadership skills or Politicking skills?**

   Select one of the following A, B, or C from below and fill in the blank.

   A. **Leadership skills**
      come first because _____

   B. **Politicking skills**
      come first because _____

   C. **Leadership and political skills are equally**
      important because _____

The prudent careerist knows that leadership skills and political skills are equally important. They are the essence of career destiny. Use the above question to show that leadership skills and politicking skills are not mutually exclusive. Many people are quick to embrace leadership skills as the way to the top of the career ladder. The same people reject the idea that politicking skills are directly connected to how people get promoted to the executive suite. In reality a leader must have at his or her disposal a variety of political skills in order to arrive at the top of the executive career ladder and maintain that position.

Career Shaping Questions

5. Sometimes when people are retiring or leaving an organization they say in a frustrated way, "After I go, I'm going to tell everything I know about this organization."

   Is exposing the politics of promotion after retirement a "no brainer" or is it an act of public courage?

   Choose A, B, or C below

   A. Exposing the politics of promotion after retirement is a "no brainer."

      Explain _____

   B. Exposing the politics of promotion after retirement is an act of public courage.

      Explain _____

   C. Other _____

When you keep something secret that could help someone else, an opportunity has been lost. A lot of people are unhappy, but remain relatively silent about the organization's unfair promotion practices while they are employed. They keep quiet for fear of retaliation from higher-ups (e.g., losing their job and retirement check). After you have left an organization it is to late to make much of a difference. The organization can write you off as a disgruntled retiree or someone who has an axe to grind. The time to make a difference is when you are in the organization. Otherwise, people question why it took you so long to tell the truth. It is an act of public courage for staff and executives to speak up and take action that will level the playing field for everyone.

Chapter 11

How to Use This Interactive Book

The real purpose of books is to trap the
mind into doing its own thinking.
C. Morley

Learn Quick and Smart

Don't expect mercy in a high speed chess game.
Stay one jump ahead of competitors by working
hard and finding ways to get pre-selected.

How to Use This Interactive Book

You're either part of the solution or part of the problem. E. Clever

The book is a virtual lightning rod for sparking healthy change. Some higher-ups feel that the book and the Multi-Cultural Promotion Track Game threaten the status quo because they clearly define problems, pose questions, and solutions that many executives prefer to avoid. This interactive book advocates a long needed deep examination of the way that career advancement politics are handled in the workplace. In many organizations the state of promotion politics is overdue for reform, clarification, and equal opportunity for access to top executive and CEO positions. Use the book as a way to draw attention to problems, issues, and concerns regarding the politics of promotion. Given that career advancement is part personal technique and part discipline, the reader should consider how to best combine the following eleven topics, in order to probe for information and secure more knowledge.

1
Use This Book To Initiate Discussions

Our senses don't deceive us; our judgement does. Goethe

Share with people the concepts, quotes, diagrams, and career shaping questions in this text. They can be used to stimulate ideas and create a precedent for discussing Career Advancement Politics in a practical and pragmatic way. In this manner, the book becomes the subject of the discussion and not an individual's personal philosophy regarding the politics of promotion. Ideally, answering the career shaping questions with the boss or with co-workers can be an effective way to give and take information while learning about the dos and don'ts of career advancement politics. As noted previously, if higher-ups are unable or unwilling to participate in open discussions, staff members can form their own discussion groups. In all cases, having the proper decorum and respect for the existence and practice of promotion politics is part of the learning process for understanding career advancement.

2

Value The Other Person's Point Of View

Knowledge is of two kinds. We know the subject ourselves,
or we know where we can find information upon it.
Samuel Johnson

The important thing in discussing Career Advancement Politics is the dialogue and exchange of ideas that one receives. While it's great to talk to people who think like you, it's better to discuss things with individuals who have diametrically opposed views. In so doing, people should be prepared to tactfully agree or disagree with people who have differing opinions or unorthodox views. The key is to learn how others think and how they arrived at their belief system.

3

Be Patient

Everything that irritates us about others can
lead to an understanding of ourselves. Carl Jung

Look for windows of opportunity, which will allow people to initiate a conversation regarding career advancement. The more discreet, natural, and individualized the opening, the easier it will be to talk about the subject. For example, individuals who have just undergone some experience regarding career advancement may be willing to discuss their situation. This may include people who have been recently hired, fired, promoted, or retired.

In other cases, an individual may have his or her own way of expressing what he or she feels is necessary or unnecessary in moving up the career ladder. In either case, the opportunity has presented itself and can be used to broaden the discussion and learning process.

4

Look For Areas You Have in Common with People

Your net worth to the world is usually determined by what remains
after your bad habits are subtracted from your good ones.
Benjamin Franklin

Many people feel they have the answer to the question of how people are promoted. Listen and learn from them. The commonalties you have with them can be the building blocks for developing relationships, rapport, and information sharing. In a conversation regarding career advancement, the ideal approach is to have people understand all three Career Advancement Models (see p. 226). To appreciate the significance of these models may take several meetings.

5

Management May Not Be Ready, Willing, or Able to Discuss the Politics of Career Advancement

We talk on principle, but act on interest. Walter Savage Landor

---

Do You Live Your Values?

When one accepts the role of leader, the person is in effect saying that he or she is willing to "walk the talk."

Example_____

Many bosses do not want to be drawn into discussions about the politics of promotion. They look for ways to avoid this topic. Talking openly about career advancement politics does not come naturally to most people. For example, some executives do not see career advancement politics as a problem worth addressing. Intellectually they may understand the problem, but emotionally they remain gloriously oblivious to it.

5

Management May Not Be Ready, Willing, or Able to Discuss the Politics of Career Advancement

Nine times out of ten, in the arts as in life, there is actually no truth to be discovered; there is only error to be exposed. Henry L. Mencken

"Walking the walk" refers to a person who lives his or her values. He or she leads by example and is open to discussing career politics. Actually, many managers are striving to position themselves for their next promotion and want to learn more about career advancement politics. They may be hesitant to talk about their needs because they don't want their political ambitions to be known. Others may feel uncomfortable discussing issues with staff, feeling that this is something that managers never do or if they do it's among themselves. Or, they feel that fraternizing between superiors and staff is never done. Obviously, all of these excuses are open to refutation. However, if the organization is ever going to move from talking about leveling the playing field to actually doing it, the process must begin with dialogue between staff and management.

Speaking Truth to Power = Fairness and Balance

It's the uncommon executive who takes time to thoroughly analyze behavior and question the organization's promotion practices. It's even more rare that an executive makes the necessary changes.
It seems that no one has been taught to talk professionally about promotion politics. Given the complexities of career politics, there will never be an easy way to begin the dialogue. If progress is to be made, the dialogue must start and continue to deal with pleasant as well as unpleasant political realities. If management does not show leadership in this area, the staff needs to pick up the topic and talk about it respectfully. When astutely done, the professionalism with which the subject is handled by staff will pique management's curiosity and cause managers to desire to become part of the change process.

6

Respect the Other Person

*The problems that exist in the world today cannot
be solved by the level of thinking that created them.*
Albert Einstein

Given that politics is here to stay and that it permeates so much
of organizational life, it must be dealt with in a way that accords the
proper deference to people and the positions they hold, especially if
they are higher-ups. This process requires one to be able to properly
sort out one's feelings and experiences before speaking. Next, one
must be able to mentally and emotionally separate the person from
the position. And deal with each of them separately. As the saying
goes, to solve the problem, focus on the problem, not the person.
Misconceptions may occur unless both parties appreciate the other's
point of view. Entering a conversation with an attitude of half-
listening or a cavalier mentality is extremely counterproductive.

7

Play and Learn
from the
Multi-Cultural Promotion Track Simulation
Game

Games lubricate the body and the mind. Ben Franklin

This fast paced critical thinking game has something important
to say about the human condition and career advancement politics in
action. People learn best those things with which they have first-hand
experience. This fast-paced, critical thinking simulation (Page 245-252)
allows participants to walk in someone else's shoes and try to make it
to the top of the organization. It can be used to generate discussion
as an example of good or bad career advancement politics. As a role
playing educational game the simulation challenges the status quo's
way of doing things. It creates teachable moments that can be used
to help someone understand the other person's universe of thinking.

8
Establish the Need
for an
Ongoing Dialogue

*It is impossible to begin to learn that which one
thinks one already knows.*   *Epictetus*

The subject of career advancement is always timely, because most people want to move up in their chosen careers. However, career advancement is just too complex and wondrous to be fully discussed in one meeting. Seek a commitment for additional group or face-to-face sessions. Use this book and simulation game as points of reference and schedule several meetings. Each meeting can be used to discuss different sections in the book or simulation game. Focus groups that examine specific parts of the promotion system can find out information, formulate questions, and create a more transparent workplace.

9
Be a Life-Long Learner

You seek problems because you need their gifts.
Richard Bach

Read and trade ideas about Career Advancement Politics with a wide range of people. Acquire as much knowledge as you can about career advancement, leadership, ethics, and critical thinking skills. Look for ways to transfer and apply these ideas and concepts from one discipline to another. This transferability is the key to creating synergistic thinking, which generates new knowledge and insights. No matter what you hear, after having talked to someone, ask yourself, "What has this person taught me about career advancement that I can use to better myself?" How can I use the information to advance my career or to safeguard my position?

10
Discuss the Politics of Promotion Without Fear

*Our problems are man-made; therefore they
can be solved by men. And man can be as
big as he wants. No problem of human destiny
is beyond human beings. John F. Kennedy*

What some people fear the most is removing fear in its many subtle and overt forms from the workplace. Some feel that if people know how things are really done, staff will leave. The truth is that many people already have a strong suspicion of how things are done and still stay with the organization. The worst thing that can happen is that people who are going to leave will leave because they already made other plans. The best thing that can happen is that people in their own way will come to terms with the realities of Career Advancement Politics and make more informed career decisions.

Discussing Promotion Politics Must Be a Priority

**The overarching goal is to find ways that move
management and staff to a new level of trust,
communication, and problem solving.**

Example _____

Take the long view of career advancement. This perspective makes it clear that finding ways to have discussions about the politics of promotion is to your advantage. Make the conversations happen and maintain a business-like composure when discussing career politics. Know how to ask questions as well as how to answer them. It's OK to ask probing questions, but know when to back off, lighten up, and not create a contentious atmosphere by keeping people on the defensive. Regroup and continue the dialogue another day. In short, be a class act because a class act is hard to follow.

11
Understand That People's Values Are Very Personal

Doubt is the beginning not the end of wisdom. Georges Iles

A person's career advancement reality is based on his or her personal perspectives and experiences with life, work, ethics, authority figures, and ambitions. People have invested a lot of time in learning to see and react to the world from their unique perspectives. They are not going to give their ideas up quickly. People change when things directly affect them. Otherwise, the status quo remains pretty much unchanged. The book and simulation game can help people stretch their comfort zones and learn how other people see things and what can be done to solve the problem.

Summary

What is wanted is not the will-to-believe,
but the wish to find out, which is the exact opposite.
Bertrand Russell

Knowing what old paradigms to discard and what new paradigms to embrace is one of the most important frontiers of career advancement. Pushing the envelope of knowledge about Career Advancement Politics can be an exhilarating act of self-awareness. It generates enlightened discussions that are essential for people who want to move ahead.

The Consummate Professional

Discussing Career Advancement Politics with dignity and professionalism is crucial for self-empowerment.

If you want the present to be different from the past,
study the past.   *Baruch Spinoza*

Summary

*People would rather live with a problem they cannot solve
than accept a solution they cannot understand.
Robert Woosley and Huntington Swanson*

Today's workforce has access to a lot of timely information regarding career development. People who are primed for career advancement are looking to move up the career ladder as quickly as possible. Having access to information empowers them to compare and contrast their career advancement philosophies and beliefs with what the organization thinks and believes. In this manner they can decide what they can or cannot live with, in terms of the politics of promotion. Thus, it is incumbent upon executives to step up to the plate and candidly discuss the politics of promotion.

Don't Pull Your Punches

**Take a long, hard look at what it takes to advance
to the executive level. Being able to openly discuss
the good, the bad, and the unfair has a direct impact
on the organization's ability to
recruit,
retain, and
promote quality people.**

The secret to effectively using this book is to be uniquely above average in the way you carry out your work. Never stop asking diplomatic as well as hard ball questions. Understand the boss's problems and how he or she defines performance and likeability - formally and informally. These are the keys to protecting your job and getting into the pipeline for executive advancement.

Chapter 12

The Multi-Cultural Promotion
Track Simulation Game

Hands-on-Training Tool

I hear and I forget.
I see and I remember.
I do and I understand.
> *Confucius*

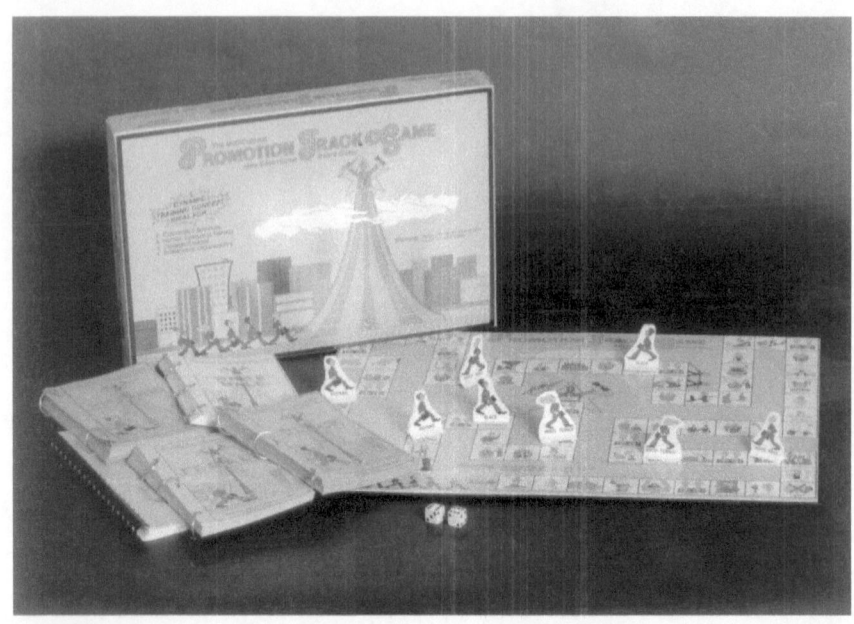

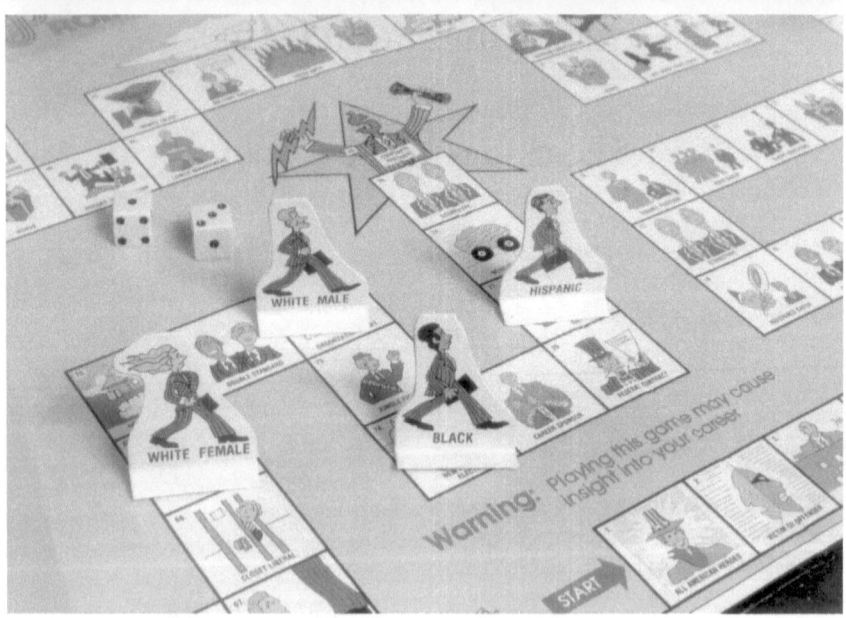

To Walk In The Other Person's Shoes
Is To See, Feel, Hear, And
Experience Life From Another Person's Perspective.
It Can Make or Break Career Advancement

The Multi-Cultural Promotion Track Game

When it comes to career advancement politics, people learn best through first-hand experiences. The educational board game is based on the premise that the more experience a person has, the more self-confidence he or she will have when meeting the real thing. The less intimidated a person is when confronted by the politics of promotion, the stronger his or her resolve will be to move up the ladder of success. Self-confidence springs from the person's inner resourcefulness and ability to analyze and make informed career decisions. Career advancement favors people who have an inside-out knowledge of the organization's strengths and blind spots. For this reason, the author has designed a fun training tool that brings to life the concepts discussed in this book. When used together, the book and the simulation provide a 360-degree view of the Politics of Promotion.

Warning:
**Playing This Game May Cause Insight
Into Your Career.**

The educational game is the is the centerpiece of a highly interactive training concept that simulates career advancement in a multi-cultural organization. As a paradigm shift, it allows people to "walk the talk" of Career Advancement Politics by role playing an Asian, African-American, Hispanic, White female or male. Just as in real life, the participants compete with one another for promotions. The simulation uses dice, script books, and the players' wit and wisdom. By developing a "felt reality," it takes participants from an awareness phase to the action level of the workplace. They become thoroughly engaged in the concept, which is played within the context of a hypothetical organization and reflects on the job perspectives. Any similarities to your organization are purely coincidental. As a result of this awareness building, players are better equipped to discuss sensitive issues in a practical way. The book and the educational game reinforce one another and provide a powerful frame of reference that can help make organizational behavior more transparent.

How The Educational Concept Works

Life is an endless process of self-discovery.   J. Gardner

Depending on the time available and the organization's needs, the simulation game can be used as a stand-alone activity or as a workshop activity. The four steps listed below are helpful in pre-positioning the program.

Step 1. Presentation (optional)
Step 2. Simulation exercise
Step 3. Workbook (optional)
Step 4. Discussion and recommendations

1. Presentation (optional)

It often takes more courage to change one's opinion than to keep it.
Willy Brandt

The facilitator delivers a presentation and identifies the learning objectives. A sample list of objectives can be found in the game instruction sheet. Presentation topics may include issues covered in this book or other material related to the topics of leadership, ethics, and cultural diversity. See the list provided below. The simulation brings the objectives to life by picking up where the presentation leaves off, e.g., players apply lessons from the text to the simulation game. Presentation is optional.

Potential Topics For Presentation

Career Advancement Dynamics	**Politics of Promotion**
Cross-Cultural Awareness	**Affirmative Action**
Preventing Sexual Harassment	**Clarification of Values**
Multi-Cultural Leadership Skills	**Organizational Behavior**
Critical Thinking Skills	**Change Process**

The simulation is very helpful when there in no one around to bring up topics that need to be discussed regarding workplace politics. Use the career development tool as a catalyst for discussing sensitive issues in a practical way e.g., workplace diversity, ethics, and management skills.

How the Educational Concept Works

2. Simulation Exercise
Nothing is so sad as the death of an illusion. Arthur Koestler

By using true to life scenarios, the game produces candid "you are there" situations. They reveal the way we play the game or ought to play the game of career advancement politics. Players learn through personal experience about the objectives presented in Step 1 (Presentation). Participants use script books to role-play Asian, African American, Hispanic, White female or male, and they compete for promotions. The scenarios in the script books produce a paradigm shift and generate critical thinking from a role reversal perspective, e.g., examining values, challenging assumptions, and analyzing organizational cultures. Written with fact and word play, the program is an educational and entertaining learning process. After the game is played the participants are placed into groups based on the role they played—Female group, White male group, Hispanic group, African-American group, Asian group.

3. Workbook (Optional)
I am strongest when I laugh at my weakness. Elmer Diktonius

Based on the role played, participants are placed into groups and analyze their experiences. Playing the game allows for role reversal. It may be the first time that a male has played the role of a female or a White male has walked in the shoes of a Black, or a Hispanic has played the role of an Asian. They complete written exercises regarding the situations they encountered and share them with the group. Sample questions:

A. What types of coping skills did you have to develop in order to survive in this organization? Apply the various career advancement models from the text and assess the promotion practices of the (game board) organization.

B. Identify the impact that good and bad stereotyping had on you.

C. Based on the role you played, what recommendations would you make to create a healthier work environment?

How The Educational Concept Works

Not everything that is faced can be changed,
but nothing can be changed until it is faced. James Baldwin

4. Discussion

Everyone is a prisoner of his experiences.
No one can eliminate prejudices-just recognize them.
Edward R. Murrow

The educational game represents the front wave of change in the way that people treat one another in the workplace. With this in mind the facilitator blends the learning objectives with responses from the groups and workbooks. Participants use color markers and large flip chart paper to identify and list their talking points for presentation to other groups. Based on the role they played and situations they encountered, the groups are encouraged to share their experiences. This reinforces insights about experiences and recommendations for improving the organization depicted on the game board.

Participants can use the career development tool repeatedly and learn from new experiences by changing roles, as they try to become CEOs, e.g., one time a participant may play an Asian, the next time a Hispanic.

Critical Thinking Objectives

To find the exact answer, one must first ask the exact question.
S. Tobin Webster

1.

What do you know now about what you didn't know? Use the educational game as a good or bad example of Career Advancement Politics. The educational game is designed to explore organizational behavior as it relates to career advancement dynamics. All of the chapters in the book can serve as a point of reference for discussing and analyzing situations presented on the game board of career advancement.

Critical Thinking Objectives

How often have I said to you that when you have eliminated the
impossible, whatever remains, however improbable, must be the truth?
Sherlock Holmes

Triangulate
Executive Career Advancement Behavior

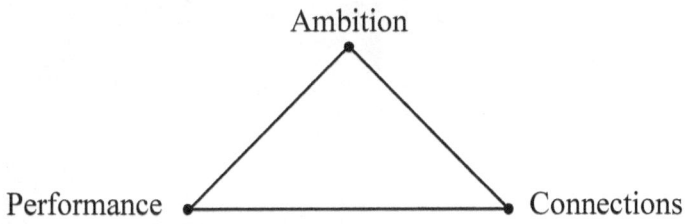

Career advancement to the top is not for the faint hearted. It takes an inquiring mind to triangulate how people and things in the organization are connected, how they relate to one another, and interact under various conditions. The educational game and book can help triangulate organizational behavior by fleshing out key career influencing factors and identifying how they impact your advancement. One of the secrets to career advancement is being able to comprehend and work with the organizational connective tissue that binds people and things together. The book and game serve as a catalyst for pin point discussions and as a reference point for parsing words, concepts, and analyzing situations. They highlight examples of good career politics and bad career politics. Together the book and game can generate ideas that help maintain a positive work environment. In many cases the recommendations for improving the organization on the game board may have application for contemporary organizations.

People who are aware of and ashamed of their prejudices are well on the road to eliminating them. Gordon Allport

---

To order the educational game contact:

LFCareer.com   Phone (559) 222 - 6307

Game opens door to communication

BY RON COLLINS

Communication is key in Venice Smith's job.

The problem is that her job as a University multicultural coordinator involves discussion of an issue that often many people are afraid to talk about.

"I've been setting up diversity interviews with people since I first came here last year," Smith says, "and most of the people I call are very apprehensive about meeting with me to discuss diversity issues."

It's Smith's job to help the MSU community understand what diversity is and why it's a good thing for MSU.

Earlier this year, Smith's search for new ways of easing the tension that often surrounds discussions about diversity led her to a game that was being used by an array of American companies in their efforts to promote diversity.

The game, called the "Multicultural Promotion Track Game," was designed specifically for corporate America. The only other university using it at the time was Stanford University in California.

"Corporate America found out that it was having real problems that weren't racially motivated but were more a problem of people not understanding or appreciating the cultural differences of others," Smith says. "They're using this game to help address the problem."

The game is similar to "Monopoly," in that players roll dice and move figures around a board.

The difference is that players are assigned to be a different race or gender than they actually are. As players move their figures along the board, they land on squares representing different career situations.

Players are then given several options to address the situation. Each option has a different outcome depending on a player's assigned race or gender.

Broadcast/Marketing/Photo - Bruce Fox

Venice Smith, multicultural coordinator, looks over the "Multicultural Promotion Track Game," a new tool to stimulate discussion and promote communication on campus about diversity issues.

"How fast, if at all, you move up the corporate ladder varies dramatically depending on your race or gender," Smith says. "It really opens a lot of eyes.

"Having people take on different roles than they are helps them to understand what it's like to be in someone else's shoes."

Smith says the game stimulates discussion and, for this reason, it's important to have a diverse group of players so that all express their points of view.

Reaction to the game from people who have played it is mixed.

"Some people find it depressing, and others find it shocking," Smith says, "but most people walk away feeling they've learned something.

"Overall, people feel comfortable playing this game because we do it in a relaxed atmosphere."

As awareness of the game increases on campus, so does the number of people wanting to play it. Smith says that people have been calling her for a chance to sign up for the next session.

To Smith, that's a good sign that the "Multicultural Promotion Track Game" may be the key that helps open the lines to better communication on the issue of diversity at MSU.

▶**CALIFORNIA LIVING**

Board game shows struggles minorities face at workplace

FRESNO (AP) — It has dice and little characters that move from square to square, but the board game Lawrence Flores devised is a lot more serious than "Monopoly."

Its purpose is indicated by this phrase on the board: "Warning — playing this game may cause insight into your career."

The "Multicultural Promotion Track Game" gives players an insight into hurdles women and minorities may have to overcome if they want to get promoted at work.

In each game, one piece represents blacks, another Hispanics, a third Asians, a fourth white women. The fifth piece represents white males, who are presumed by the rules to be the dominant force in most offices.

"Sometimes, students argue over who will play the white male, assuming he is going to win," Flores says. "It is tilted in his favor, but he does not always win. It depends on how you play the role."

The pieces representing white males won just half the

time when Flores split members of a graduate social worker class at California State University-Fresno into four groups, and each played a separate game. Pieces representing an Hispanic and a white woman were the other winners.

The rolls of the dice mean players need some luck to reach the winner's circle — the corporate presidency with its perks of power and pay.

But the ethnic group and/or sex they're playing also makes a major difference. Their options on each square are limited or enhanced by information on that square coupled with material they read in a booklet linked to that ethnic group or sex.

Some students feigned the attitudes they thought people of the ethnicity they represented might adopt.

"I don't want to play," Mary Momen, a white woman who was playing a black piece, said after a bad move. "I'm not going anywhere."

"The game's not over yet," Flores said.

The game also produced

Associated Press
Lawrence Flores rolled the dice and came up with the Promotion Game.

some strange exchanges. Arby Dedmon, a white woman in real life, told Frank Renteria, an Hispanic playing a white woman: "You're a very aggressive female."

Heather Compton, a white woman playing a Hispanic, won her game even though she was sure at one point, "I'm going to get canned now."

Compton refused to file a discrimination charge, causing fellow players to accuse her of "selling out" to get to the top.

In a bull session afterward, several students seemed cynical about how ethical issues are handled in the job world.

"As long as we were selling out, we were advancing," said Rosalyn Estrada, an Hispanic who played a black game piece.

"Basically, to advance you had to kiss corporate butt or you'll be a janitor," Compton said.

"I held to my values, so I didn't go anywhere," Renteria said.

Others felt they had to make bad personal choices to advance.

"Doors were open to me, but I sacrificed my health and my family to stay at the top," said

Suzanne Rodriguez, an Hispanic who played the role of a black male. "Employers praised me."

Flores said such attitudes are common as players try to win the promotion game.

"I've seen people start with squeaky clean values and see that they're getting behind, so they put a spin on their values," he said. "They thought they could get ethical when they get to the top."

Flores invented the game in 1982 to give his classes a feel for how stereotypes and other forms of discrimination can affect their chances of getting ahead. But he also wants the game to give insight into methods that can be used in seeking promotions.

"I want them to look at what they need to develop both personally and professionally to move up the career ladder," Flores said. "Secondly, it helps them learn how to better analyze the organization with emphasis on promotions."

Flores said he found that students rarely are taught anything in college about the stresses workers face, such as fear and favoritism.

Associated Press
Kristy, Garavello, Suzanne Rodriguez and Richard Valenzuela sample the game.

About The Author

Lorenzo Flores, Ph.D. is the premiere speaker in the field of Career Advancement Dynamics. He has pioneered research into the Theory and Practice of Promotion Politics. He feels that Career Advancement skills are on the same level of importance as Leadership and Management skills. His work sets the gold standard for discussing and analyzing the politics of career advancement.

In addition to this book, he has designed a fun learning game: The Multi-Cultural Promotion Track Game. The educational tool has earned national recognition. He holds a Ph.D. in Urban Studies, Master of Public Administration, and Master of Social Work from the University of Southern California. Undergraduate degree in Police Science/Corrections from San Jose State University. Background experience includes: Director of Social Work, probation officer, college instructor, and Viet Nam Era Veteran.

LFCareer.com   Phone (559) 222-6307

Seminars by Lorenzo Flores, Ph.D.

Dynamics Of Career Advancement:
How To Understand The Politics Of Promotion

I Want To Get Promoted, But I Don't Want To Play The Game

Top 10 Ways To Survive and Thrive In The Workplace

How To Effectively Work With The Boss

Teamwork: Maintaining A Healthy Work Environment

New Supervisors: Managing Today's Challenges

Leadership Styles: Developing Extraordinary Skills

Ethics: Fact, Fiction or Flexible

Ten Myths And Ten Truths Of Career Advancement

Cultural Diversity: The Multi-Cultural Promotion Track Game

Cross Cultural Mentoring For Success

Leadership Strategies Of General Pancho Villa

Critical Thinking Skills: The Professional Edge

Dealing With Difficult Co-workers

Conflict Management Skills

Executive Mindset: From Clean Politics to Dirty Politics
In Three Seconds

Keynote Address and specially designed workshops available.

Bibliography

Bacon, Sir Francis, Daniel B. Baker, Power Quotes, Visible Ink Press, Canton, MI 1992

Reston, James, The Wit and Wisdom of Politics, Chuck Henning, Fulcrum Publishing Golden, CO 1992

Lincoln, Abraham, www.Leadershipdevelopment.com 12-10-03

Flores, Lorenzo, Dynamics of Career Advancement, AuthorHouse, Bloomington, IN 2005

Peters, Laurence J, Peters Quotations, William, Morrow and Company, Inc. NY 1977

Disraeli, Benjamin, Chuck Henning, Fulcrum Publishing Golden, Colorado 1992

Flores, Lorenzo, Dynamics of Career Advancement, AuthorHouse, Bloomington, IN 2005

Genesis 1, 30A, Subparagraph VIII, Robert Townsend, Further up the Organization Prennial Library Harper & Row, Publishers, NY 1988

Flores, Lorenzo, Dynamics of Career Advancement, AuthorHouse

Manske, Fred, Jr. www.Leadershipdevelopment.com 12-10-03

Voltaire, Francois, Peter's Quotations, Laurence J. Peter William, Morrow and Company, Inc. NY 1977

Mahoney, David, Jr., Quotable Business, Louis E. Boone, Random House NY 1992

Six Minutes News Program 1-18-04

Grove, Andrew S, The Big Book of Business Quotations, Ultimate Business Library, Bloomsbury Publishing Plc, NY 2003

Channing, William Ellery, www.Leadershipdevelopment.com 12-10-03

Waterman Robert H., The Renewal Factor, Bantam 1987

Marquis, Don, Leonard Roy Frank, Random House Webster's 2000 NY

Schopenhauer, Arthur, www.Great-quotes.com 10-14-03

Bardwick, Juidith M., The Plateauing Trap, American Management Assoc. 1991 NY

Maimonides, Mose, Lewis D. Eigen and Jonathan P. Siegel, American Management Association 1991 NY

Eldridge, Paul, Leonard Roy Frank, Random House Webster's 2000 NY

Brinkley, David, Chuck Henning, Fulcrum Publishing Golden, CO 1992

Atkinson, Brooks, Leonard Roy Frank, Random House Webster's 2000 NY

Carrington, Alexis, Life 101, John-Rogers and Peter Mcwilliams, Prelude Press, 1991 Los Angeles, CA

Bancroft, George, Laurence J. Peter, William Morrow & Company Inc. NY 1977

Watson, Thomas Sr., Lewis D. Eigen and Jonathan P. Siegel, American Management Association 1991 NY

Buffett, Warren, The Big Book of Business Quotations, Bloombury Publishing Plac 2003

Morgan Pierpont, John, Quotable Business, Louis E. Boone, Random House NY 1992

Shakespeare, William, Whitney, John and Packer, Tina, Power Plays, Simon and Schuster NY 2000

Bruyere, Jean de la, Leonard Roy Frank, Random House Webster's 2000 NY

Davis, Elmer, Louis E. Boone, Random House NY 1992

Hubbard, Kin, Leonard Roy Frank, Random House Webster's 2000 NY

Holmes, Oliver Wendell, Chuck Henning, Fulcrum Publishing Golden, CO 1992

Dunne, Finley Peter, Leonard Roy Frank, Random House Webster's 2000 NY

Peter, Laurence J., William, Morrow & Company Inc. 1972 NY

Kennedy, John F., Leonard Roy Frank, Random House Webster's 2000 NY

Bacon, Francis, William Morrow and Company, Inc. NY 1977

Holmes, Oliver Wendell, Leonard Roy Frank, Random House Webster's 2000 NY

Geus, Arie P. de, Harvard Business Review, March/April 1988

Locke, John, Lewis D. Eigen and Jonathan P. Siegel, American Management Association 1991 NY

Rayburn, Sam, Leonard Roy Frank, Random House Webster's 2000 NY

Culberston, Ely, Chuck Henning, Fulcrum Publishing Golden, Co 1992

Waterman, Robert H., Lewis D. Eigen and Jonathan P. Siegel, American Management Association 1991 NY

Plato, Louie E. Boone , Random House NY 1992

Voltaire, Leonard Roy Frank, Random House Webster's 2000 NY

Lasch, Christopher, Leonard Roy Frank, Random House Webster's 2000 NY

Trahey, Jane, The Big Book of Business Quotations, Basic Books, New York 2003

James, William, Louis E. Boone, Random House NY 1992

Connolly, C., Laurence J. Peter, William Morrow & Company Inc. 1972 NY

Benn, Stanley I., Wasserstrom, Today's Moral Problems (Macmillan, 1975)

Edwards, Bob, Laurence J. Peter, William Morrow and Company, Inc. NY 1977

Shakespeare, William, Louis E. Boone, Random House NY 1992

Barada, Paul W., Lewis D. Eigen and Jonathan P. Siegel, American Management Association 1991 NY

Anonymous, Lewis D. Eigen and Jonathan P. Siegel, American Management Association NY

Manfred F.R. Kets de Vries and Danny Miller Lewis D. Eigen and Jonathan P. Siegel, American Management Association NY

Bonaparte, Napoleon, www.great-quotes.com 10-14-03

Gilbert, W. S., Leonard Roy Frank, Random House Webster's 2000 NY

Disraeli, Benjamin, Leonard Roy Frank, Random House Webster's 2000 NY

Disraeli, Benjamin, Chuck Henning, Fulcrum Publishing, Golden, CO 1992

Gaylin, Willard, The New York Times, October 7, 1977

Norris, K. Norris, Laurence J. Peter, William Morrow & Company Inc. 1972 NY

Montesquieu, Baron de, Laurence J. Peter, William Morrow and Company, Inc. NY 1977

Ellington, Duke www.allthesecrets.8m.com 10-15-03

Holmes, Sherlock, www.10Ktruth.com 10-14-03

Baker, Russell, Leonard Roy Frank, Random House Webster's 2000

Beal, Louise, Laurence J. Peter, William Morrow and Company, Inc. NY 1977

Fosdick, Henry Emerson, www.Leadershipdevelopment.com 10-16-03

Stephanopoulos, George, Leonard Roy Frank, Random House Webster's 2000

Allison, Mary Ann and Melville Dalton, Lewis D. Eigen and Jonathan P. Siegel, American Management Association 1991 NY

Deal, Terrence E. and Allan A. Kennedy, Lewis D. Eigen and Jonathan P. Siegel, American Management Association 1991 NY

Lewis, Roy and Rosemary Stewart, The Boss (Phoenix House, 1958)

Dalton, Melville, Lewis D. Eigen and Jonathan P. Siegel, American Management Association NY

Eastland, James, Lewis D. Eigen and Jonathan P. Siegel, American Management Association NY

Bruyere, J. De., Laurence J. Peter, William Morrow & Company Inc. 1972

Coleridge, Samuel Taylor www.great-quotes.com 10-15-03

Whittier, John Greenleaf www.thoughtsforyou.com 10-16-03

Forbes, Malcolm, Lewis E. Boone, Random House, NY 1992

Runyou, Damon, Louis E. Boone, Random House NY 1992

Esar, Evan, Leonard Roy Frank, Random House Webster's 2000

Kierkegaard, Soren, Finlayson, Andrew, Questions That Work, American Management Association 2001

Zand, Dale E., Lewis D. Eigen and Jonathan P. Siegel, American Management Association NY 1991

Flores, Lorenzo, Dynamics of Career Advancement, AuthorHouse, Bloomington, IN 2005

Armour, Richard, Laurence J. Peter, William Morrow & Company Inc. 1972 NY

Hobbes, John Oliver www.allthesecrets.8m.com 10-15-03

Macaulay, Lord, Power Quotes, Daniel B. Baker, Visible Ink Press 1992 Canton, MI

Kissinger, Henry A., Louis E. Boone, Random House NY 1992

Performance Science Corp. Advertisement, 1986

Conrad, Joseph www.Great-quotes.com 10-15-03

Korda, Michael, Lewis D. Eigen and Jonathan P. Siegel, American Management Association NY 1991

Frost, Robert, Lawrence J. Peter, William Morrow and Company, Inc. NY 1997

Nader, Ralph, Lewis D. Eigen and Jonathan P. Siegel, American Management Association NY 1991

Thoreau, Henry David, www.10K Truth.com 10-15-03

Einstein, Albert, Leonard Roy Frank, Random House Webster's 2000 NY

Aristotle, www.BrainyQuotes.com 10-14-03

Ginsberg, Allen, Leonard Roy Frank, Random House Webster's 2000 NY

Galbraith, John Kenneth www.KenFran.Tripod.com 10-15-03

Viries, Peter de, Leonard Roy Frank, Random House Webster's 2000 NY

Brilliant, Ashleigh, Woodbridge Press Publishing Company 1980 Santa Barbara, CA

Telleyrand, Charles Maurice de www.Brainyquotes.com 10-15-03

Whitehead, Alfred, Lewis Eigen and Jonathan P. Siegel, American Management Assoc. NY 1991

Rohn, Jim, Carden Gwen, Yount, American Media Mini Mags. Inc, Boca Raton FL 2003

Goheen, Robert F., Leonard Roy Frank, Random House Webster's 2000 NY

Peters, Laurence J. www.Quotationspage.com 10-16-03

Gibran, Kahlil, White, Rolf, The Great Business Quotations 1986, Dell Publishing New York 10017

Boltnick, Srully, The Corporate Steeplechase (Facts On File, 1984)

Kay, Alan, Lewis D. Eigen and Jonathan P. Siegel, American Management Association NY 1991

Roosevelt, Theodore, Lewis D. Eigen and Jonathan Siegel, American Management Association NY 1991

Sergeant Preston of Yukon, Lewis D. Eigen and Jonathan Siegel, American Management Assoc. NY 1991

Baker, Russell, Leonard Roy Frank, Random House Webster's 2000

Whitehead, Alfred North, Chuck Henning, Fulcrum Publishing Golden, CO 1992

Von Eschenbach, Marie Ebner, www.Quotationspage.com 10-16-03

Bruce, Lenny, Leonard Roy Frank, Random House Webster's 2000 NY

Boren, James H., Leonard Roy Frank, Random House Webster's 2000 NY

Thoreau, Henry David, Leonard Roy Frank, Random House Webster's 2000 NY

Dewey, John, Lewis D. Eigen Jonathan P. Siegel, American Management Association 1991 NY

Favoritism, Nepotism, Racism, Websters New World Dictionary Second College Edition

Bebel, August, Daniel B. Baker, Visible Ink Press, Canton, MI 1992

Einstein, Albert www.BrainyQuotes.com 10-16-03

Horton, Thomas R., Lewis D. Eigen Jonathan Siegel, American Management Association 1991 NY

Nietzche, Friedrich www.BrainyQuote.com 10-16-03

Disney, Walt www.BrainyQuote.com 10-16-03

Iapoce, Michael www.BrainyQuote.com 10-16-03

Kerr, Alphonse, Laurence J. Peters, William Morrow and Company, Inc. New York 1977

Bemar, Amy, Lewis D. Eigen and Jonathan P. Siegel, American Management Association 1991 NY

Hancock, Mal, Leonard Roy Frank, Random House Webster's 2000 NY

Hubbard, Elbert www.BrainyQuote.com 10-15-03

Tosi, Henry L. Lewis D. Eigen Jonathan Siegel, American Management Association 1991 NY

Beaumarchais, Pierre de, Leonard Roy Frank, Random House Webster's 2000 NY

Flores, Lorenzo, Dynamics of Career Advancement, AuthorHouse, Bloomington, IN 2005

Martin, Bill, Louis E. Boone, Random House NY 1992

Argyris, Chris, Harvard Business Review September/October 1986

Meacham, Merle L., Laurence J. Peter, William Morrow and Company, Inc. NY 1977

Hubbard, Elbert, Lewis D. Eigen and Jonathan P. Siegel, American Management Association NY 1991

Roosevelt, Theodore, Lewis D. Eigen and Jonathan P. Siegel, American Management Association NY 1991

Durocher, Leo, Leonard Roy Frank, Random House Webster's 2000 NY

Navratilova, Martina, Louis E. Boone, Random House, NY 1992

Cook, Marv, www.Sportshollywood.com 10-17-03

Steinbenner, George, Louis E. Boone, Random House NY 1992

Durocher, Leo, Leonard Roy Frank, Random House Webster's 2000 NY

Will, George F., Leonard Roy Frank, Random House Webster's 2000 NY

Rose, Pete, www.quoteworld.org 10-17-03

Broun, Heywood www.BrainyQuote.com 10-16-03

Rupp, Adolph, Louis E. Boone, Random House New York 1992

McCarthy, Eugene, Leonard Roy Frank, Random House Webster's 2000 NY

Gizzard, Lewis www.quoteworld.org 10-16-03

Baker, Russell, Leonard Roy Frank, Random House Webster's 2000 NY

Custer, George Armstrong, Urban Legend Magazine Week 8 www16.brinkster.com 10-17-03

Blake, William www.Great-quotes.com 10-15-03

Luce, Clare Boothe www.Great-quotes.com 10-15-03

Disraeli, Benjamin, Lewis D. Eigen and Jonathan P. Siegel, American Management Association 1991 NY

Churchill, Winston, Leonard Roy Franks, Random House Webster's 2000 New York

DeBono, Edward www.positiveatheism.org 10-16-03

Galbraith, John Kenneth, Leonard Roy Frank, Random House Webster's 2000 NY

Machiavelli, Niccolo, Chuck Henning, Fulcrum Publishing Golden, CO 1992

Flores, Lorenzo, Dynamics of Career Advancement, Author House, Bloomington, IN, 2007

Keillor, Garrison, Leonard Roy Frank, Random House Webster's 2000 N Y

Eliot, T.S. www.Leadershipdevelopment.com 12-10-03

Pascale, Richard T. and Anthony G. Athos, Lewis D. Eigen Jonathan P. Siegel, American Management Association 1991 NY

Adenauer, Konrad, Chuck Henning, Fulcrum Publishing, Golden CO 1992

Lewis D. Eigen and Jonathan P. Siegel, American Management Association 1991 NY

Galbraith, John Kenneth, Leonard Roy Frank, Random House Webster's 2000 NY

Korda, Michael, Leonard Roy Frank, Random House Webster's 2000 NY

Rochefoucauld, Francois de la, Leonard Roy Frank, Random House Webster's 2000 NY

Kerrey, Robert, Chuck Henning, Fulcrum Publishing, Golden, CO 1992

Rochefoucauld, Francois de la, Leonard Roy Frank, Random House Webster's 2000 NY

Rochefoucauld, Francois de la, Leonard Roy Frank, Random House Webster's 2000 NY

Bierce, Ambrose, Power Quotes Daniel B. Baker, Visible Ink Press 1992 NY

Lapham, Lewis H., Leonard Roy Frank, Random House Webster's 2000 NY

Peters, Laurence J, William Morrow and Company, Inc. NY 1977

Sage, Russell, Lewis D. Eigen Jonathan P. Siegel, American Management Association 1991 NY

Connolly, Cyril, Leonard Roy Frank, Random House Webster's 2000 NY

Nixon, Richard M., Life 101, John-Roger & Peter Mcwilliams, Prelude Press, 1991 Los Angeles, CA

Lao-tzu, Life 101, John-Roger & Peter Mcwilliams, Prelude Press, 1991 Los Angeles, CA

Edwards, Bob, Laurence J. Peter, William Morrow and Company, NY 1977

Edison, Thomas Alva, Louise E. Boone, Random House 1992 NY

Hoffer, Eric www.Allthesecrets.8m.com 10-15-03

Lichtenberg, Georg Christoph www.Allthesecrets.8m.com 10-15-03

Kemelman, Harry, Laurence J. Peter, William Morrow and Company, Inc. NY 1977

Lord Beveridge, Leonard Roy Frank, Random House Webster's 2000 NY

Erhard, Ludwig, Chuck Henning, Fulcrum Publishing Golden, CO 1992

Emerson, Ralph Waldo, Roget's International Thesaurus, Thomas Y. Crowell Company New York 1962

Bittle, Less www.Leadershipdevelopment.com 10-16-03

Tyger, F. www.Leadershipdevelopment.com 10-16-03

Holmes, Oliver Wendell Sr. www.Allthesecrets.8m.com 10-15-03

Secrets of Effective Leadership www.Leadershipdevelopment.com

McLaughlin, Mignon, Leonard Roy Frank, Random House Webster's 2000 NY

Drucker, Peter, Louis E. Boone, Random House NY 1992

Bendaly, Leslie, Games Teams Play, McGraw-Hill Ryerson 1996

Luckman, Charles, Louise E. Boone, Random House NY 1992

Freud, Sigmund www.Kornea.com 10-14-03

Lippman, Walter www.Great-quotes.com 10-15-03

Clopton, Richard, Laurence J. Peter, William Morrow & Company Inc. 1977 NY

Gandi, Mohandas K. www.Kornea.com 10-14-03

Sinclair, Upton, Leonard Roy Frank, Random House Webster's 2000 NY

Churchill, Winston, Life 101, John-Roger & Peter Mcwilliams, Prelude Press, 1991 Los Angeles, CA

Russell, Bertrand www.Brainyquotes.com 10-16-03

Steinbeck, John, Lewis D. Eigen Jonathan P. Siegel, American Management Association 1991 NY

Lord Macaulay, Daniel B. Baker, Visible Ink Press 1992 Canton, MI

Frankl, Viktor, Life 101, John-Roger & Peter Mcwilliams, Prelude Press, 1991 Los Angeles, CA

Romney, George, Louis E. Boone, Random House 1992 New York

Talleyrand, Charles Maurice de www.BrainyQuotes.com 10-15-03

Shakespeare, William, Leonard Roy Frank, Random House Webster's 2000 NY

Whitehead, Alfred North, Laurence J. Peters, William Morrow and Company Inc. NY 1997

Holmes, Oliver Wendell, Chuck Henning, Fulcrum Publishing, Golden CO 1992

Twain, Mark, Chuck Henning, Flucrum Publishing, Golden, CO 1992

Benchley, Robert, Leonard Roy Frank, Random House Webster's 2000 NY

Disraeli, Benjamin, Chuch Henning, Fulcrum Publishing, Golden, CO 1992

Argyris, Chris, Harvard Business Review, September/October 1986

Goodman, Ace, Leonard Roy Frank, Random House Webster's 2000 NY

Flores, Lorenzo, Dynamics of Career Advancement, AuthorHouse, Bloomington, IN 2005

Brilliant, Ashleigh, Woodbridge Press Publishing Company, 1980 Santa Barbara, CA

Wilde, Oscar, Leonard Roy Frank, Random House Webster's 2000 NY

Will, George, Chuck Henning, Fulcrum Publishing Golden, CO 1992

Ruskin, John, www.Allthesecrets.8m.com 10-16-03

Russell, Bertrand www.Quotationspage.com 10-16-03

Disraeli, Benjamin, Chuck Henning, Fulcrum Publishing Golden, CO 1992

James, Williams, Leonard Roy Frank, Random House Webster's 2000 NY

Berne, Eric, Games People Play, Transactional Analysis, Grove Press, Inc. N Y 1964

Lamott, Anne, Leonard Roy Frank, Random House Webster's 2000 NY

Commager, Henry Steele www.Wisdomquotes.com 10-16-03

Morley, C., Laurence J. Peter, William Morrow & Company Inc. 1972 NY

Cleaver, Eldridge, Power Quotes, Daniel B. Baker, Visible Ink Press, 1992 Canton, MI

Goethe www.Kornea.com 10-14-03

Johnson, Samuel, Laurence J. Peters, William Morrow and Company, Inc. NY 1977

Jung, Carl, Life 101 John-Roger & Peter Mcwilliams, Prelude Press 1991 Los Angeles

Dryden, John, Lewis D. Eigen, Johnathan P. Siegel, American Management Association 1991 NY

Landor, Walter Savage, Leonard Roy Frank, Random House Webster's 2000 NY

Mencken, Henry L., Lewis D. Eigen Jonathan P. Siegel, American Management Association 1991 NY

Einstein, Albert, www.Kornea.com 10-17-03

Franklin, Benjamin www.Brainyquotes.com 10-16-03

Epictetus www.Quotationspage.com 10-16-03

Bach, Richard www.Kornea.com 10-16-03

Iies, Georges, www.Kornea.com 10-17-03

Lewis E. Boone, Random House 1992 New York

Woosley, Robert and Swanson, Huntington, Lewis D. Eigen Jonathan P. Siegel, American Management Association 1991 NY

Gardner, J., Laurence J. Peter, William Morrow & Company Inc. NY 1997

Brandt, Willy www.allthingswilliam.com 10-16-03

Koestler, Arthur www.Greatest-quotation.com 10-16-03

Diktonius, Elmer www.Garofaloland.com 10-15-03

Baldwin James www.Great-quotes.com 10-16-03

Murrow, Edward R. www.wisdomquotes.com 10-16-03

Webster, Tobin S. American Management Association 2001

Holmes, Sherlock, Lewis D. Eigen Jonathan P. Siegel, American Management Association 1991 NY

Allport, Gordon www.Tawjihe.com 10-15-03

Selected Reading Bibliography

Albright, Mary, and Clay Carr. *101 Biggest Mistakes Managers Make*. Upper Saddle River, NJ: Prentice Hall, 1997.

Arden, Paul. *It's not How Good You Are, Its How Good You Want To Be*. London: Phaidon, Press, 2003.

Axelrod, Alan. *Office Superman: Make yourself Indispensable in the Workplace*. Philadelphia: Running Press, 2004.

Barry, Douglas. *Wisdom For a Young CEO*. Philadelphia: Running Press 2004.

Basic Books, *Movers & Shakers: The 100 Most Influential Figures in Modern Business*. London: Bloomsbury 2003.

Berne, Eric. *Games People Play*. Jackson, TN: Grove Press, 1964.

Cox, Allan. *Inside Corporate American*. New York: St. Martin's Press 1986.

D'Alessandro, David F. *Career Warfare*. Columbus, OH: McGraw Hill, 2004.

Davis, George, and Glegg Watson. *Black Life in Corporate America*. New York: Anchor Books, 1985.

Dickens, Floyd, Jr., and Jacqueline B. Dickens. *The Black Manager*. New York: AMACOM, 1991.

Dubrin, Andrew, *Winning Office Politics*. Upper Saddle River, NJ: Prentice-Hall, 1990.

Evans, Gail. *Play like a Man, Win Like a Woman*. New York: Broadway Books, 2000.

Gallwey, Timothy W. *The Inner Game of Work*. New York: Random House, 2000.

Gilbert, Brad. *I've Got Your Back*. New York: Penguin 2004.

Harragan, Betty Lehan. *Games Mother Never Taught You*. New York: Warner Books, 1977.

Harvard Business Essentials. *Coaching and Mentoring*. Boston: Harvard Business School Publishing, 2004.

Hawley, Casey. *100+ Tactics for Office Politics*. Hauppauge, NY: Barrons Educational, 2001.

Josefowitz, Natasha. *Path to Power*. Boston: Addison-Wesley, 1990.

Heffernan, Margaret A. *The Naked Truth: A working woman's Manifesto on Business and What Really Matters*. 2004.

Kaplan, Robert. *Warrior Politics*. New York: Vintage Books, 2003.

Kennedy, Marilyn Motes. *Office Politics*. New York: Warner Books 1981.

Kennedy, Marilyn Motes. *Office Warfare*. New York: Fawcett Crest, 1985.

Koch, Richard. *The 80/20 Individual*. New York: Random House, 2004.

Michaleson, Gerald A. *The Art of War for Managers: 50 Strategic Rules*. Cincinnati, OH: Adams Media, 2001.

Michaelson, Gerald, and Steven Michaelson. *Sun Tzu for Success*. Cincinnati, OH: Adams Media, 2003.

Maccoby, Michael. *The Gamesman*. Bantam Books, 1976.

Murrell, Kenneth L., and Mimi, Meredith. *Empowering Employees*. Cincinnati, OH: Adams Media, 2003.

Nader, Ralph, and William Taylor. *The Big Boys*. New York: Pantheon, 1986.

Pardoe, Blaine. *Cubicle Warfare*. Pima Publishing, 1997.

Robbins, Stephen, P. *The Truth About Managing People*. Upper Saddle River, NJ: Prentice Hall, 2003.

Citin, James, M., and Richard A. Smith. *The 5 Patterns of Extraordinary Careers*. Budapest, Hungary. Esaress Holding, Ltd. 2003.

Stalk, George Lachenauer. *Hard ball: Are You Playing to Play or Playing to Win?* Harvard Business School Press, 2004.

Trump, Donald. *The Way to the Top*. New York: Crown Business, 2004.

V. *The Mafia Manager*. New York: St. Martin Press, 1996.

Whitney, John O., and Tina Packer. *Power Plays*. New York: Simon & Schuster, 2002.

Whyte, William H., Jr. *The Organization Man*. New York: Clarion, 1956.

Index

X

Y

Z

www.ingramcontent.com/pod-product-compliance
Lightning Source LLC
Chambersburg PA
CBHW030250290526
45785CB00001B/33